What people are saying about ...

Chris

"No one blends self-deprecating hilarity and spiritual profundity like Mark Steele. *Christianish* is everything we've come to love about his writing: It's entertaining, it's challenging, and it's completely devoid of cheese."

Jason Boyett, author of *Pocket Guide to the Afterlife*

"Mark Steele is no Jeremiah. It's a good thing, because we'd have to kill him. Funny, incisive, and wise, Steele calls us (along with himself) to account for all our fakery and get on with the serious business of (gulp) living like Jesus."

Patton Dodd, deputy editor of PurposeDriven.com and author of *My Faith So Far: A Story of Conversion and Confusion*

"Look out! Mark Steele is in the temple and he's flippin' tables! Mark always has something funny to say about Christianity, but this book is as convicting as it is hilarious. He continues to use his comedy as a metal detector that finds 'the real stuff' under the rubble. In between references to Boss Hogg and *Cannonball Run 2*, you might actually reexamine your whole approach to following Jesus."

Cory Edwards, writer and director of *Hoodwinked*

"Sometimes when I'm feeling depressed and lonely I like to imagine Mark Steele is my best friend, and we are walking through a grassy meadow in the warm sunshine. As the butterflies float by and bunnies bound ahead of us, Mark cheers me up by offering gentle wisdom and hilarious life stories about his journey on this earth. Now that I have a copy of his new book, this dream of mine can become a reality. I cannot recommend *Christianish* highly enough as a thoughtful and humorous look at some of the most serious truths of a Christian's walk with the Lord. You'll laugh, you'll cry, you'll buy the book … hopefully, if you are reading this, you already have. If not, what are you waiting for?"

Stephen McGarvey, executive editor of
Crosswalk.com and Christianity.com

CHRISTIANISH

what if we're not really
following Jesus at all?

MARK STEELE

David C Cook®

transforming lives together

Christianish
Published by David C. Cook
4050 Lee Vance View
Colorado Springs, CO 80918 U.S.A.

David C. Cook Distribution Canada
55 Woodslee Avenue, Paris, Ontario, Canada N3L 3E5

David C. Cook U.K., Kingsway Communications
Eastbourne, East Sussex BN23 6NT, England

David C. Cook and the graphic circle C logo
are registered trademarks of Cook Communications Ministries.

All Scripture quotations, unless otherwise noted, are taken from the *Holy Bible,
New International Version*®. *NIV*®. Copyright © 1973, 1978, 1984 by International
Bible Society. Used by permission of Zondervan. All rights reserved; MSG are taken
from *THE MESSAGE*. Copyright © by Eugene H. Peterson 1993, 1994, 1995,
1996, 2000, 2001, 2002. Used by permission of NavPress Publishing Group.

LCCN 2009928006
ISBN 978-1-4347-6692-2
eISBN 978-1-4347-0039-1

© 2009 Mark Steele

The Team: Andrea Christian, Susan Tjaden, Jaci Schneider, and Karen Athen
Cover/Interior Design: Amy Kiechlin
Cover Photo: iStockphoto, royalty-free
Exhibit Illustrations: Eric Lee

Printed in the United States of America
First Edition 2009

1 2 3 4 5 6 7 8 9 10

052709

To Morgan, Jackson, Charlie, and David.
May you follow Jesus regardless of the
world in which you live.

christian*ish*

What if we're not really following Jesus at all?

mark steele

In everyday life, when one chooses to acknowledge another, it is the equivalent of gesturing toward that person as if to point out which end of the compass is north. Not so in a book. In a book, to acknowledge someone is to sum up in very few words the substantial importance said individual has played in the book writer's life. To this end there are a great number of individuals I could acknowledge for various and sundry reasons, though I will not. I could, for instance, acknowledge my wife, Kaysie, for her undying love and support as well as for her willingness to suppress the urge to insert my hand into a scalding-hot George Foreman Grill each time I drive a lengthier path to a destination than the path she would have chosen. I could acknowledge my father, whom I will call Dad, for allowing me to abandon baseball at an early enough age to kick-start my writing career. I could thank him for encouraging me to write those spec *Moonlighting* episodes while I blared Tears for Fears from my room. I could. I could acknowledge my mom, who gave blood, sweat, and tears so that I could have a Christian education, thanking her especially for bringing some rationale and perspective to said curriculum so that my schooling was not skewed to Tri-State Regional Competition levels. I could acknowledge my children: Morgan, Jackson, Charlie, and brand-spanking-new baby David (though it's a bit too early for spankings), simply because I love them, and their foibles provide great literary material. I could acknowledge my pastor, Roger Nix, for keeping me sane. I could acknowledge my business partner Kevin Anderson and the entire Steelehouse team for making art-as-business a joy. I could acknowledge my brothers and brother-in-law for deflating my sometimes-swelled head. I could acknowledge Eric Lee for the amazing illustrations that he deciphered out of my chicken scratch, or my editor Andrea Christian for reminding me to write up some acknowledgments. Let's face it: I could acknowledge some of the everyones of importance, significance, or influence in my life. But I won't.

Instead I acknowledge them all. For they all drive me every single day to ditch the *–ish* and instead genuinely follow Jesus Christ.

I also acknowledge Jesus Christ.

Mark Steele
January 2009 (ish)

i am Christian*ish*

At approximately three o'clock, on an otherwise uneventful afternoon, random disaster landed in my living room, scarring my wife's affenpinscher permanently. In a collision of arbitrary calamity—the sort of incident one reads about in a James Frey memoir but does not believe—my wife accidentally cut off our dog's tongue with a pair of grooming scissors.

Off.

Tongue.

Grooming scissors.

The dog was named Scout in honor of the little girl in *To Kill a Mockingbird*, though he is neither a girl nor currently inside any fancy books. It must first be respectfully noted that the dog's tongue is his talent. It is his method of showing affection, and he wields it with a flourish like the caricature artist on the boardwalk waves pastel chalk before sketching your oversized head on the body of a minuscule muscleman. Scout's lick was his love. It was all he really knew how to do—that tongue was his Sistine Chapel.

Of all the human beings who could have fathomably been the bearer of this specific catastrophic misstep toward my dog—a cutlery juggler, a careless balsa whittler, the lady who runs the paper shredder at Kinko's—the least likely and the worst emotional choice is the human who actually did the deed. That would be my wife, Kaysie.

The reason Kaysie is the worst choice as the cause of this particular accident is because there is not a human soul on the planet who loves the dog more. In fact the atrocity occurred during an act of kindhearted affection. Kaysie was grooming Scout with great precision and detail—prettying him up because, after all, he is named after a girl. She was only slightly distracted by the fact that her back was aching, she was about to leave town for five days, and she had just received word that a loved one had passed away. Still, she forged ahead with the necessary grooming. She took a clump of his doggie hair between the blades, and then—just as she squeezed—Scout whipped his face around, jamming his tongue in the middle of the shears themselves.

SHINK.

The rest—as you would imagine—was gross.

Scout was rushed to the vet, where they angrily asked how this could have happened. *I don't know how this happened! The dog was licking an envelope while I accidentally slipped it in the paper-shredder. What do you think happened?!* The vet quickly gave him ten stitches. Ten. I reiterate this because the vet also reiterated this, making sure we fully understood that Scout was a tiny dog and that he should have never been subjected to such terror. Ten stitches, the vet insisted, were ten stitches too many.

He chewed them all out overnight. The determination was made in the morning that Scout would need to have the dangling participle removed altogether. The tongue-ectomy was performed. A fourth of his slobbering member was omitted. From then on he yelped with a lisp. It's a good thing my name is Mark.

So Kaysie felt horrible and she shouldn't have, because it wasn't her fault. It was just the rotten way everything sort of fell together in light of the chaos that was going on around her, mixed with the flitting nature of the dog. But that doesn't change the fact that it did indeed happen. It doesn't change the fact that Scout's tongue is now gone for good.

I understand Kaysie's guilt and grief because I have also played a part in someone's catastrophe. Several someones in fact. I have played a part in many needful things being removed.

The scissors I wielded were not tangible. They were different things in different seasons of my life: the cutlery of my inconsistent ways, my sarcastic tongue, and my resistance to maturity. In too many moments, when I knew full well that someone was watching, I selected selfishness—to make decisions in a manner that would benefit myself most of all. I tossed about my acidic words like Agent Orange on a rice field. I snubbed my nose at others whose sin or failure was simply a nuanced variation of my own. I aimed for godliness as an idea, but was quick to snag the do-over of grace when my intentions proved faulty. I judged. I condemned. And I thought it was okay because the people of the church were still impressed with me.

But the world was watching.

Funny. I always thought my attempts at godliness wouldn't make all that much difference to the world. In light of the mammoth sunshine of Christ, I was at best a tiny blip of a moon. Miniature and reflective. Barely a dust mite in light of that massive star. Unfortunately that tiny moon is capable of blocking out the light of the sun almost entirely. It's called an eclipse, and it is what happens when the vastly smaller moon is hovering too close to the observer and in front of the sunlight. Yes, most nights we moons reflect the light, claiming its grandeur as our own—but occasionally, through a sudden collision of random happenstance, we make the sun seem to completely disappear.

This should come as no surprise to me because my own faith journey was marred by a number of moons blotting out the light. One religious leader in particular had many profound God-ideas that transformed me—but he also used to ridicule my weight on a regular basis. He was joking, of course, but due to my ongoing neuroses regarding weight gain, I was never able to hear any truth out of his lips past the moon of that repeated statement. This was unfortunate he had some very good things to say.

This knee-jerk reaction to criticism and insults developed a defense mechanism inside of me. Ironically this defense was my wit. If I could insult and get a laugh before the other person, then I never had to be called fat or weak or worthless again. So I manufactured the very same set of scissors that had cut me. Kindness had been ripped from my person and replaced with something akin to coarseness. A leathery coating of intellect and cleverness that would hide the ugly fear and mask it with uglier pride. This was my weapon—and I daily saved myself by harming everyone else.

The root of the problem—and the real damage—is that while I lived in this dysfunction, I called myself Christian.

I never really liked the name Christian. I was told it meant "little Christ," and as a thirteen-year-old, that sounded (at best) presumptuous and (at its basest) freakishly cocky beyond all measure. In all honesty I didn't want to be a little Christ. It seemed both insulting to God and too much pressure for me. I didn't want to be a souvenir of Jesus. I didn't want to be His homeboy—a bobblehead version you buy at the gas station that cheapens the real deal. I wanted instead to be a follower of Christ. I'd heard that phrase bandied about and I thought it sounded accurate. And cool. I would vastly prefer to be an arrow pointing to the Great Question, rather than have someone mistake me for the answer.

My take on the matter was unfortunate because the truth actually lay somewhere inbetween. No, I do not believe Jesus desired for me to be mistaken for Him. He did not intend for my singular actions to be the sole picture of who He truly is. But He did and does fully urge me to pursue being one of the many earth-pictures that cause people to see Him at work in their lives.

This was a risky move for God. By making each and every one of us who calls himself "Christian" an active parable of His love, He is hazarding the chance that some (or even one) of us won't take that symbolism very seriously. Somehow in the scheme of the passage of time, we have placed the issue of "example of Jesus" into the hands of evangelical religion as a whole, living as if "together, somebody's got everything covered." But this is not reality. Reality beckons a weak-link theory: that even a singular one who calls himself little Jesus, and yet lives the opposite, damages the whole caboodle—and in effect damns the world that is watching.

In a crude analogy, we're advertising Coca-Cola by saying it tastes like turpentine and then growing antagonistic towards those unwilling to take a swig.

And yet God took the risk anyway, because He knows that the other end of the spectrum is also true. As much as it damages the reputation of Christ for those who call themselves Christians to live the antithesis of His teachings—on the flip side it makes quite a statement when a flawed human makes a right decision with nothing in it for himself other than taking a stand for Christ. It is the single most tangible way to prove the intangible. This was God's plan: that when the world looks at each of us, they would not simply see a follower of Him. In some miraculous and unexplainable way, God knows that when the world stares at a flawed human who somehow occasionally chooses holy and unhuman actions, they see a picture of Jesus. It is the one true arrow that God's grace allows us each to be. A conduit for a relationship between someone else and God. This is why He took the risk. This is why He took the risk on me.

But something happened along the way.

Somewhere along the road of offense and defense, I stopped being a little Christ and instead began filling out the application that I had labeled Christian. It was not a definition based on the actual namesake, but rather on those who frequent the clubhouse. And in the midst of being an American Christian among all the other American Christians, I stopped truly searching the nuances of who Christ *was* and *is* in order to fully grasp what a little Christ might, indeed, *act like.* Certainly I soaked in the Word of God in seasons. I knew the key stories—the greatest hits: the miracles, the Beatitudes, the Passion Week, and whatnot. But I chose not to apply the reality of all the truth in between His words and actions into my own behavior. I allowed Jesus to seep into my church world—but not my relational world, my romance world, my business world, my creative world, my habits, my mouth.

I read His words.

I learned His words.

But I did not fully belong to Him.

Because of this I became a sort of half-breed. I segregated myself—splitting my soul into two segments: one that would openly serve Jesus and one that would secretly protect myself. I became like people I deemed my-kind-of-godly instead of becoming like Jesus. I pursued Christian success instead of pursuing Christ. I spoke witty insults as commonly as profound prayers. And in the process I called myself a Christian without ever becoming a little Christ at all. I became something else.

Not truly Christian—but rather, merely Christian*ish*.

As a church community it is time we asked ourselves a startling question: What if we're not really following Jesus at all?

Our Christian intention has sharp edges. It has the ability to mold and shape, but also to stab and permanently damage. We have been wagging these blades carelessly for far too long while distracted by some very non-Christlike habits, behaviors, and dysfunctions. Because we are unable to notice our own distraction, we keep on waving our razors, impressed with our own cutlery skills until we suddenly find ourselves the benefactors of unintentional but irreversible wounds. And I don't simply refer to wounds made by a few. They are made by us all. By you. By me—by Mark Steele. Yes, we do our best to remedy these wounds, calling our efforts misunderstood and leaning on God's grace—in hopes that we can pick up off the floor that which we amputated and use the excuse that we handed it back. But it's not enough, not even close to enough.

THE WRONG ROAD

How did modern evangelicalism lose its balance? How did some behavior fall into an accountability category while other distractions remained unaddressed and therefore socially and religiously acceptable? For me personally my efforts had become more centered on how to cope with my own dysfunctional life, and less concentrated on what it really means to follow Jesus. I was more than off balance. I was traveling the wrong road completely.

To this end I recall how poor my sense of balance was when I first began Rollerblading. My roommates and I used to lace up and blade through the Saturday streets of downtown Tulsa while blaring Spin Doctors from our Walkmans. The first time we adventured as such, I expected myself to have zero difficulty. I had, after all, gone to the roller rink with Harold Johnson every Saturday afternoon from age nine all the way through to age twelve. In Columbus, Georgia, this weekly intersection of pinball, couple-skating, and gorging ourselves on banana-flavored Now and Laters was the hot ticket. And I could do it all: dodge cones, speed race, or skate in reverse if the *Dukes of Hazzard* theme was playing to inspire me. How different could these newfangled Rollerblades be from those old four-wheel jobs?

The answer? Different enough.

Where I had spent a half decade of my youth learning to stop on my toes, the Rollerblade had no such mechanism. This greatly affected the way I stopped in downtown Tulsa. Rollerblades were designed to stop by turning my feet into a V. This was difficult to master, so instead, I just kept throwing my body into lampposts.

At least seventeen times.

I literally stopped the momentum of my body by throwing myself into lampposts on purpose. My reasoning? Less bodily damage than throwing myself into moving automobiles.

After eight months of working with the Rollerblades, I was no longer a novice. I had mastered the stop, the sharp turn, and every move necessary to adventure my favorite rollerway: Riverside Drive. Riverside is about six blocks of nonstop sidewalk alongside the river, with no roadway interruptions. It is a great place to get your jog on, your Rollerblade on, your freaky-skintight-biker-pants on. (I don't wear them myself for fear of skin overflow.) One fateful day I decided to take a long roll down to the very end. This was a relatively big deal because I had never Rollerbladed the yonder forbidden turns, though I had biked farther. So I parked my car and began blading south, whipping past elderly speed-walkers and children on bikes with training wheels—thinking them fools for their slowness and feeling the clean, cold pavement whisk by underneath my rubber wheels.

As I rapidly approached the point where I had previously always turned around, I decided to forge onward, but I knew from my experience biking the path that this would require bravery. I was gaining momentum, and I knew that to keep going meant that I would have a sharp ninety-degree turn to my right followed by an immediate sharp ninety-degree turn to my left underneath a bridge. These were intense moves at this speed and I was not certain I was up for the challenge.

But I determined to go for it.

The curve came, and I leaned my body down to the right—*fwoosh*—and made the first turn. Then, sure enough, I shifted my body weight just as precisely the other way—*sweesh*—and made the second turn. I could feel the wheels trembling, my leg muscles straining—it was possible that I was about to bite it. But I did not. Because I had trained. I knew well that the road in front of me was going to hold massive twists and turns and so I had prepared myself to handle them appropriately.

What I did not realize was that, underneath the bridge in the shadows, the pavement turned to gravel.

My wheels hit the tiny stones and I flew—literally flew several yards, arms outstretched like a flying squirrel—into sand and pebbles. I felt them embed into my hands, chest, and legs. That sensation of flesh ripping. You know that sensation.

Not awesome.

I lay there, moaning. I staggered up, knowing that once the wind hit all of the scrapes and open wounds, I would be doomed. The wheels on one of my blades were now crooked, and my shorts were ripped. Oxygen did its thing, and suddenly all sorts of places on my body were bleeding.

As I stood there in great pain and pouring plasma like a *Monty Python* sketch, I realized how wrong I had been to think myself prepared. I had deceived myself into thinking that the way to travel a unique road was by simply getting better and better at Rollerblading. The problem was that this road was not a Rollerblading road at all. To traverse it would not require a refinement of the old method. It would require a completely different method altogether.

I skated with one leg while dragging the other a full mile and a half back to my car. It was mosquito season and a small nation of them suddenly realized the picnic of my body. I looked like one of those bee-keepers in the *Guinness Book of World Records*, but without the sense of accomplishment. Every time I approached an elderly speed-walker or a training-wheel child, their eyes grew wide in horror. One mother shielded her child's face from looking directly at me and, if I am not mistaken, assumed I was a horseman of the coming apocalypse. I prob-ably should have said "help" to one or more of these people. Instead, to each of them, I uttered the same word:

"Sorry."

Once home I stood in my shower while one of my roommates threw large cupfuls of hydrogen peroxide at my body and I bit down on a pencil.

Great pain. Great scars.

And I had thought I was prepared.

This is the difference between Christian*ish* and Christ-follower. We have trained ourselves to cope well on a Christian*ish* path: a path where we please the right godly people and don't feel guilt when our failings are seen by the world at large. Yes, our methods work on this path—but it's the wrong path. It's not the approach to Jesus that we are supposed to take—that we are created to take.

So we fall into confusion over why life doesn't work and why our faith doesn't feel right and why nothing true is coming from our so-called Christianity. We attempt to fix it by refining our current method. But here's the catch: The method won't work on the *right* road, because it is a method built for the *wrong* road.

We cannot change the dysfunction of our Christian walk by simply trying to become better at the wrong we are already living.

We must switch roads. And in switching, we must discover the new method of living that truly works on the right road.

There is only one way for me to discover the right way to travel the right road.

The way is not a church.

The way is not an ideology.

The way is not a Christian.

The way is Jesus.

In my path of becoming functional in a dysfunctional faith, I crashed and burned quite often. I became and remained the lukewarm that gets spit out. The vomit to which the dog returns. The goat that was separated from the sheep. I nodded and even verbalized *amen* at each and every one of those stories, tsk-tsking internally at the target of the moral, never once interpreting that the antagonist might just be me.

I was at risk of becoming the one at the pearly gate whom the very Jesus I thought I was serving says He never knew. I lost the plot altogether, grasping at the path toward eternity that fit most nicely into my temporal goals.

FROM CHRISTIAN*ISH* TO CHRIST-FOLLOWER

So the question begs: How does the transformation begin? From Christian*ish* to Christ-follower. What is the road? And what is the method? It is certainly a painful road. A gravel-laden path that requires going back to the very beginning and digging deep into Jesus' words and actions during the time He walked and breathed on planet Earth.

When you look at the New Testament from the Jesus perspective, it breaks down quickly into eleven key components of His history:

1. How He came into the world.
2. How He was tempted.
3. How His enemies responded to Him.
4. How He ministered to the common man.
5. How He made His living.
6. How He responded to His enemies.
7. How His friends responded to Him.
8. How He loved.
9. How He performed miracles.
10. How He died.
11. How He left.

The truth is here—not merely in the verses we have memorized, but in the manner in which the Savior spent His days. For me to become the true definition of a Christian, it will require breaking His thoughts down—and being willing to transform my own behavior into what I discover. It will require facing the music—and then doing something about it. It will require unlearning and baby steps. I have no idea what that sort of experiment will entail.

But I'm going to find out.

I now set out to find the right road.

The functional method.

I will be a Christ-follower.

And leave the stench of Christian*ish* behind for good.

26

christianish

Christian*ish*   Christ-follower

Exhibit a

1.   Have you found your Christian efforts leading to dysfunctional lifestyle patterns? Describe how.

2.   Does the idea of attempting to do the right thing when you are actually on the wrong road resonate with you?

3.   When you search your motives, do you find that you are trying to please Christ, or do you find instead that you are attempting to earn your Christianity?

4.   How does the following comment relate to your life: *"I segregated myself—splitting my soul into two segments: one that would openly serve Jesus and one that would secretly protect myself. I became like people I deemed my-kind-of-godly instead of becoming like Jesus. I pursued Christian success instead of pursuing Christ."*

scandalous   1

Nineteen months are all that separate my two older sons, Jackson and Charlie. In practically every way, one is the antithesis of the other. They both have their strengths and weaknesses, but smash them together and they fill out the other's weak spots, becoming one practically perfect human being. Of course, the scattered remains that are left would be a bit messy. In other words, they complete one another, either as a right example or as a wrong one—their choice.

Charlie is seven and Jackson just turned nine, which means their choices—at least for the time being—might skew a bit ornery. A few months ago I walked upstairs to turn off our daughter Morgan's light for bedtime. It was later than usual and a good hour after the boys had been put to sleep (which means something different for children than it does for pets). They had been told to go right to bed. Unconsciousness isn't really something that can be demanded of a child, but I—like millions of parents before me—made the attempt anyway. As I opened Morgan's door to check on her, I caught the two

boys in her room. They ceased midplay, frozen, and stared at me—
deer in the headlights. They stood in the middle of her bedroom, a
clump of Legos squeezed in each fist. They gaped with wide-eyed
guilt on their faces for about three solid seconds. And then they ran
like mad wildfire through the adjoining bathroom. I heard the scurry
of feet on linoleum, followed by the bounce of springs and the flip-
flop of covers as they scrambled into bed.

Reasoning doesn't enter into the equation all that much at the
ages of seven and nine. For some reason not only was the rationale to
sprint away and dive into bed considered a good idea, but the identi-
cal urge to flee the scene hit both brothers at the same time.

I sauntered through the hall to their bedroom (the longer path
than the bathroom route by about eleven inches) and creaked open
the door. Each was in his own bunk, feigning sleep. And so the
cover-up began.

ME: *Boys?*

They attempted to rouse themselves from their faux slumber, "What?
Huh?"

ME: *Were you out of bed and playing in Morgan's room?*

A beat. A moment of pause. And then—both—simultaneously ...

BOYS: No.

Certainly I sympathize with the gut instinct of the cover-up. It is the defensive urge of the male, not to mention the mischievous prepuberty male. In later stages of life, it will be replaced in turn by hormones, rage at injustice, and unnecessary snacking. Throughout my own young journey, I was on the punishment end of the cover-up multiple times.

It felt ironic to finally be on the other side.

ME: *No? You were NOT in Morgan's bedroom?*

Sweat trickled down their tiny foreheads.

BOYS: Nope. No. Nope.
ME: *Just now? Like, fifteen seconds ago, you were NOT holding Legos in Morgan's room?*
BOYS: (Slightly more hesitant than before) Noooo.
ME: *(I paused for dramatic effect.) Well—I saw you.*

Not since the Noahic Era have the floodgates burst open so abruptly. The words "I'm sorry" rat-a-tat-tatted out of their mouths repeatedly in a fusillade of desperate penance.

ME: *I know you are sorry, but you lied. You know what the punishment is for lying.*

I'm fairly certain there were a couple of "yes, sirs" uttered amid all the slobber and snot.

ME: *Go downstairs. You're each going to get one spank.*

Yes. My wife and I believe in spanking. Not grab-your-knees-while-the-back-of-your-eyeballs-rap-against-your-brain spanking. But certainly a recognizable sting that serves as a tangible reminder of *why* the punishable incident was a bad idea. We want our kids to have a sensory reinforcement that sin is not such a preferable option. It always astounds me when parents don't believe in appropriate spankings, because the world spanks people every day—especially the people who didn't receive any as a child. Personally I would rather feel a short-term sting than the sort the Internal Revenue Service doles out.

Of course, an appropriate spanking is exactly that. Just enough to sting—and definitely on the derriere. And of course, the act is attached to teaching and forgiveness and a walking through of the issue so that it leads to reconciliation and change and love.

That's the pretty version.

The boys weren't seeing the benefits just yet.

Jackson and Charlie have a very different approach to the news of an impending spanking. Charlie just stares. Wide-eyed. His brain immediately begins clicking and whirring. Within fifty seconds he orchestrates a mental plan of how best to charm his way through the incident with minimal pain. By a sheer act of will and a reasoning through percentages, he determines swiftly that playing the situation down will cause it to end with only a slight portion of hurt to his person.

Jackson destroys everything within his wake.

Not literally. He doesn't throw things or flail. But within a small eight-inch radius the planet implodes. Jackson takes the news that he will receive one spank the way most react in a house fire. He hugs his favorite belongings close to his body while screaming and rolling on the floor.

I ushered Jackson into the spanking chamber (our bedroom) first as I knew that the twenty-two solid minutes it would take to actually deliver the one spank would be an epic purgatorial wait (and hence, bonus lesson) for Charlie.

The reason a Jackson spanking can take so long is because we don't believe in wrestling our kids into the spanking. There has to be the moment of surrender. Charlie can fake surrender like the best of them—but Jackson? Not so much.

ME: *Lean over, son.*

JACKSON: I CAN'T! I NEED A GLASS OF WATER FIRST!

ME: *You can have a glass of water after your spank. It will take ten seconds.*

JACKSON: I MUST HAVE A GLASS OF WATER FIRST! I'M THIIIIIRSTY!

ME: *You cannot have a glass of water until after your spank.*

No one tells a father he is going to be put in a position to say these sorts of irrational things.

ME: *You're stalling. Let's just get the punishment over with.*

JACKSON: NOW I HAVE TO GO TO THE BATHROOM!

ME: *What?*

JACKSON: YOU CAN'T SPANK ME BECAUSE I'LL
          PEE! I HAVE TO GO TO THE BATHROOM
          FIRST!
ME: *You can go to the bathroom after I spank you. We*
          would be finished already …
JACKSON: YOU'LL WHACK THE PEE OUT OF ME!
ME: *I promise I won't whack the pee out of you.*

See. Irrational things.

Of course, this is when Jackson moves from delay tactics and transitions into physical blockers. As I lean him over and pull back the spank stick, all sorts of appendages start flailing about spastically like Muppet tails, blocking the punishment trajectory. I've never seen the kid move so fast as he does when he strategizes a spank block.

ARM   HAND   ARCH BACK!!
  ARM, FOOT, FOOT, HAND   FINGERS
PUSHING AWAY ARM   HAND, DOUBLE-HAND,
    FOOT   HAND   BOTH FEET (wow)!
ARM, HAND   ARCH!

The kid is Mister Miyagi-ing me, suddenly Jean-Claude Van Damme, blocking every attempt to close the deal. He won't play football, but *this* he can do.

I finally settle Jackson down.

ME: *Jackson, I'm not going to fight you. You have to decide*
          that you're going to accept the consequences for what

> *you've done. You've fought me so long, that now you're*
> *going to get—*

(Wait for it.)

ME: *—two spanks.*

Son.
Of.
A.
Gun.

I had no idea what the kid had in him. He began to writhe and weep and gnash his teeth. I'd never seen gnashing—but it's actually very impressive. I believe he may have even utilized sackcloth. The boy just flat-out wailed like he was being branded with a hot iron. To the neighbors, it must have sounded like I was stunning him with a police Taser.

And then Jackson moved away from delaying and blocking—to step three: blame.

JACKSON: IT'S MORGAN! SHE'S THE LIAR!! SHE LIES
           ALL THE TIME!
ME: *Who are you and what have you done with my*
           child?
JACKSON: MORGAN LIES! SHE LIIIIIIIIIIIES!
           MOOHAHA!
ME: *All right, son. For that, you're now going to receive—*

Somewhere, between the bedrock layers of our planet, a mush-
room cloud was forming its power, readying itself for a self-imploding
FOOM! Tension built, and a roar and a rumble began to build just
beneath the crust of the earth.

ME: —*three spanks.*

And that is when Jackson vomited.

Seriously.
He barfed.
He wasn't sick to his stomach or coming down with a virus.
The boy got so worked up over three spankings that he literally
upchucked everywhere.
He blew chunks all over the proceedings.
As a father you can't help but debate your own discipline tactics
at this point.
I helped him wash up and then cooled him down with a cloth.
He began to settle. After a few moments I addressed him.

ME: *You okay?*
JACKSON: I told you I needed to go to the bathroom.

Against all of Jackson's hopes and dreams, the regurgitation ses-
sion did not replace any of the punishment, and I forged ahead with
the three spanks anyway. The beauty of Jackson is, though he fights
you all the way, you know where he stands. When the punishment is
over, Jackson is quick to reconcile, huddled and sobbing in my arms.

At that moment, after the pain, he is truly repentant. And he always comes out the other side changed.

Amid all of this excitement, Charlie sat waiting in the hall.

For twenty solid minutes. Hearing the sounds of torrential screams and human retching.

He sat, stone. Eyes like nickels on a plate of fine china.

Needless to say, Charlie walked in, bent over, and received his one spank in about six seconds flat.

Immensely accommodating.

But alas, not nearly as life-changing as Jackson.

It's harder to tell whether or not Charlie truly changes, because Charlie knows how to charm. During that same spanking, he sat near Kaysie and spoke to her as Jackson's sobs and moans were muffled behind the bedroom door.

> CHARLIE: I'm not gonna do anyfing Jackson is doing when I go get MY spanking.
>
> KAYSIE: *You're not, huh?*
>
> CHARLIE: Nope. I'm gonna walk wight in and jus' get spanked.
>
> KAYSIE: *That's a good idea, Charlie.*
>
> CHARLIE: I do not wike it when Daddy spanks me.
>
> KAYSIE: *I'll bet you don't.*
>
> CHARLIE: I wike it when you spank me.

This piqued Kaysie's interest and she hesitated before asking nonchalantly–

> KAYSIE: *Oh really? Why?*

CHARLIE: Because when Daddy spanks me, it hurts—but
           when you spank me, it does not—

Charlie's gaze finally met Kaysie's. The realization of the privileged information spilling out of his mouth occurred to him. He stared.

CHARLIE: I pwobably should not have told you dat.

Kaysie smiled pleasantly.

KAYSIE: *Tell you what, son. From now on we'll let Daddy do*
          all your spankings.

Charlie sighed.

CHARLIE: Yep. I definitewy should not have told you dat.

So there is an inherent difference in the way Jackson deals with disappointment and in the way Charlie deals with it. Yes, Jackson goes off the deep end, revealing his scars and putting his emotions in front of a microphone—but at least the microphone tells the rest of us what we need to know. Jackson wrestles his flesh to the ground— and he does so in public. That's how we know the transformation is real. I know that his repentance is true because I witness his internal journey from resistance to acceptance firsthand.

Charlie? Well, you don't always know with Charlie. Charlie is good at seeming fine. He keeps his deepest feelings close to his chest.

And the rough stuff? You could go a very long time without Charlie allowing anyone to see the rough stuff. The result is an engaging and personable child—everyone's best friend—though you don't always know what's really going on inside there.

Charlie positions and decorates himself instead of getting messy and raw. In this same way that we cannot see Charlie's true repentance and feelings, we as a Christian culture disguise the ugly, bury the past, and soak the dirty laundry in perfume. We do it as an effort to put our best foot forward, believing that "faking good" ministers more than "revealing bad." We have an emotional need to seem holier than all the "thous" we encounter while fitting in to the perfect flawless world of those who side-hug us on the way to the sanctuary.

We delay. We block. We blame.

We cover up.

And we somehow believe that this delivers a better impression of what it means to serve Christ. We believe that seeming the Stepford Wife makes us some sort of recruitment tool. But the truth is, we have done more damage to the world's impression of Jesus by feigning inaccurate perfection than we could ever cause by allowing those who don't follow Christ to see us wrestling our sins and flaws to the ground.

SCANDALOUS HISTORY

Many cite Matthew 5:48, "Be perfect, therefore, as your heavenly Father is perfect," as a reason to make ourselves look good. But that verse doesn't have anything to do with fakery. It is a call, instead, to spiritual maturity. And maturity owns up to the truth. Others refer to Jesus and how it was His holiness that truly ministered. This, of course, is true. But we too quickly forget that His holiness ministered most powerfully as it stood side-by-side with His humanness. And never was His humanness more on display than in His birth.

Jesus revealed the rough stuff with the very way He first came into the world.

It seems to me that the first sentence in the first telling of the Son of God entering into this world would be glorious and filled with holy hyperbole. Not so. Instead we get a few pragmatic words: "A record of the genealogy of Jesus Christ." This is merely a preamble to the names that follow—names that expose Christ's lineage. The first chapter of Matthew fires the names off *bam, bam, bam*: so-and-so was the father of whatcha-ma-call-him—never taking the smallest breath, diving headlong into historic minutiae until *ZING!* Verse seven delivers the whopper—the first specific detail mankind received about the family Jesus comes from:

> *David was the father of Solomon, whose mother had*
> *been Uriah's wife.*

Uriah? Wasn't he the guy David had killed? Murdered after David slept with his wife? That guy? Why on earth, out of all the admirable people in Jesus' lineage—and for that matter, all the honorable traits of David—why is this bucket of family dirt given the first and greatest mark of attention? A golden opportunity missed. Here the ultimate history book had the option of paving a red carpet lined with paparazzi before Jesus, publicizing the elitist line

He came from and urging the public down to its knees in awe. This was the proof: that Jesus came from the lineage of the favorite king, the man after God's own heart—David. But instead of applauding this fact, chapter one in Matthew pauses to remind the reading audience that this great King David whose line led to the Savior—this beloved ancestor of Jesus Christ—was a man of great failure and greater scandal.

Matthew started his history book with tabloid fodder. Why?

Because just like you and me, Jesus came from a scandalous history. But unlike you and me, Jesus was not afraid for the world to know and remember that scandal. As a matter of fact, He welcomed it.

We all come from something scandalous. Perhaps those who came before us, perhaps the lives we lived before we lived for Christ, perhaps some aspect of our current lives. But in modern Christianity we have somehow deluded ourselves into believing that priority one is to eradicate this reality.

We bury. We pretend. We deny to others and ourselves.

And even worse—when the opportunity arises to actually come clean with the soiled spots of our life history—we instead make believe everything is, and always has been, a series of either perfect, fine, or no big deal. And in so doing, we make ourselves into the very fakers we detest. We somehow convince ourselves that this is what Jesus would want: a wiped-clean facade. A steam-pressed, white-cotton, buttoned-down church shirt.

We live the rough stuff—sin, hardships, our scandalous histories—but we keep it silent. We believe it to be a lapse in faith to actually comment on the rough stuff or give it reference. We assume that exhaling the rough stuff somehow gives it more power, so we smile and wave and praise the Lord that everything good is permanent and everything not-so-good had zero effect on us. We have a terrible habit of skipping the rough stuff.

I do this too. And I don't understand why.

I look at the way Jesus entered this world and I see very quickly why it was important for Him to make mention of His scandalous history. It softened the blow for the shame and disgrace that would accompany Him into the world. It was as if Jesus said, *I know the manner in which I am born is going to start the rumor mill flowing, so I might as well give it a head start*. And what rough stuff it was:

- a mother pregnant before even married
- a father who almost broke off the engagement
- parents who make their decisions based on angel dreams
- a cousin born of the elderly
- a birth in an animal barn
- adoration from astrologers
- a birth that prompts the murder of hundreds of other infants

Let's just say that if you brought all these needs up during a prayer meeting, the family would be ostracized forever before the first syllable of *amen*.

The truth is this: Jesus experienced rough stuff before the age of five in ways you and I could never imagine. We consider Christ's sufferings and we picture Him at the age of thirty-three, but the beatings go all the way back to the birth canal.

THE ROUGH STUFF

How did we take this life picture and somehow misconstrue it to mean that if we just believed in Jesus, our lives would be wealthy, prosperous, and happy? Jesus doesn't promise that. Jesus says that many great things will come to those who follow Him, but He also promises a whole lot of lousy.

And here's the key: The lousy isn't rotten. The lousy isn't sin. The focus of your life is not supposed to be dodging lousy.

Because lousy is life.

And lousy is important.

It is in the rough stuff where we truly become more and more like Christ, because it is amid the lousy where we experience life on a deeper level. With intense pain comes the opportunity to love more richly. With disappointment comes the push towards selflessness. Neither of those come with pleasant because pleasant breeds boredom. And boredom is a moist towel where the mung beans of sin sprout. Life following Christ is not supposed to be a ride. It's supposed to be a fight because there is a very specific villain—and if we don't fight, he wins. If our Christianity aims only for pretty and pleasant and happy and rich, the Enemy becomes the victor.

But there is another just-as-important reason that we should embrace the rough stuff.

Not only because Jesus did.

And not merely because it is important.

We must embrace the rough stuff because for far too long Christians have skipped the rough stuff. We have pretended it does not exist in order to speak into existence a more promising present. But there is a massive dilemma when the Christian*ish* skip the rough stuff.

Real life doesn't skip the rough stuff.

And those who do not yet follow Jesus know this. Their lives don't skip the rough stuff and they know good and well that your life doesn't skip it either.

So while we as a microcosm of faith have been busy naming and claiming, yearning for a better bank account and more pleasant pastures, and ignoring the fact that lousy exists—the world watches.

And when they watch, they see the truth:

- *Life doesn't skip the rough stuff.*
- *We say that our lives do skip the rough stuff.*
- *Therefore we are liars.*
- *Or—at absolute best—we don't understand real life at all.*

The world is looking for Jesus, but they don't know they are looking for Jesus because they believe they are looking for truth. You and I know that truth *is* Jesus. But them? They do not know that truth is Jesus because you and I are supposed to be Jesus—and you and I couldn't look less like the truth.

For decades our focus has been completely skewed. In the eighties our passion was prosperity, never noticing that the only wealth that is important to Jesus is a wealth of love and compassion for those around us. In the nineties we were branded by righteous indignation, and Christianity became a political term that meant we were anti more things than we were pro. In the new millennium the postmodern set poured out bitterness and disappointment on the church of our parents, disregarding everything the previous generation built, only to construct the same thing with hipper color palettes and larger video screens. We still worship what we want our lives to feel like more than we worship Jesus. We still major on the minors, debating whether the book of Job is literal or parable when we should be out there pulling people out of the rough stuff. We still spend more money on self-help books than we give money to help others. We have become a club—a clique. A group that is supposed to be a perfect picture of the Father—but instead just acts like a bunch of disgruntled orphans.

And we wonder why no one wants to be a Christian.

We've got to do some serious redefining of what that word means.

I am in the same boat. I am guilty as charged for all these crimes. I look back on my life and I see more times than not that I wish someone did not know I was a Christian. Why? Because my unkind words and bad behavior probably did more damage than good to the reputation of Jesus. Yes, this is spilled milk—but the longer we resist cleaning it up, the more sour it will smell.

The root, of course, comes down to the why.

Why do we as Christians strive for extremely temporal things and call them Jesus? As a people group we are currently defined by the modern world as unloving and unwilling to gain a better understanding of any individual who is not already a Christian. These characteristics have absolutely nothing to do with Jesus. They are petty and selfish. They are Christian*ish*. And yet they are our very own bad habits. Why? Don't we mean well? Don't we want to live for Christ—to share His love with those around us? Don't our mistakes stem from our frustration with the state of society? With what we perceive as the rebellion of modern mankind against the ideology of God?

Actually—that is the core of the problem. The world is broken. Completely broken. What we neglect to accept is that we are broken also.

We each come from damaged goods and scandalous histories and then pretend those negatives have no effect on us. The result equals a sea of followers of Jesus who can't properly see or hear Him beyond the chaos of our own lives. So instead of following Him, we say we are following Him while actually following a combination of Him and our own chaos. Sometimes we get it right, sometimes we get it wrong, but most of the time it is a mixture of the two. Just enough of God to make a difference. Just enough of ourselves to leave a questionable aftertaste.

So the world sees that God is real—but at the same time, something doesn't quite sit well with them about Him. What is the negative common denominator?

The navel-gazing.

We are supposed to act as if everything is perfect, but deep down we know nothing quite is. So our silent, desperate prayer is also a stare. A constant internal eyeball on the broken shards of ourselves. Deep down most of us feel unglued—in pieces—longing for our Christian zealousness to turn to superglue. We feel that if we just do enough, act out the right formula, all the pieces will melt and coagulate like Robert Patrick in *Terminator 2*. That we will not only become whole, but indestructible. So we wall up our compassion and act shatterproof to a world at large while inside we are falling to pieces.

And we believe this reveals Jesus.

The great news is that Jesus looks down on us with the same tender compassion that He has for the rest of the world. He sees our pain. He sees our scandal. He knows what we are desperately trying to do, and He wants us to succeed.

But there is a realization that we must first accept.

We will never become indestructible by staring at our pieces.

We are not supposed to become indestructible. Untouchable. Safe.

And we aren't supposed to be staring at our own pieces at all.

Because when we stare at our own pieces, we cannot see the solution.

We only find the solution when we stare instead into the eyes of Christ—and in those eyes see the reflection of the hurting world.

We know this, but every gut instinct tells us to shout out, "I CAN'T! How can I help a hurting world when I can't even figure out how to glue back the broken pieces that make up my life?!" This is when Jesus changes our perspective. This is when He says softly …

- *You are not pieces.*
- *You are my piece.*

The Christian*ish* approach is to see our lives as irreparable shards—always striving for the glue. But that pursuit is fruitless. Because God did not put your glue in you. He did, however, make you the glue for someone else.

Our lives are not shattered pieces. This whole world is a broken puzzle—and each of us fits next to those around us.

YOU ARE THE GLUE

My favorite television show is ABC's *Lost*. The masterminds Damon Lindelof and Carlton Cuse have constructed a vast mythology where none of the bamboo strands make any sense until the day they eventually become a basket. Yes, I adore the convoluted structure and the peel-back-the-layers mystery of it all, but more importantly I appreciate the fact that the strands in that basket … are people.

The beauty of *Lost* is that these characters were marooned on an island with no foreknowledge of any of the others. They each carry their own bruises, scandals, and broken pieces onto this island. What they do not know is that each is the glue for someone else's piece. Sawyer has the information Jack needs from his dead father. Locke knows where Sayid's long-lost love lives. Eko knows that Claire's psychic was a phony. Each one is the ghostbuster to what haunts the other—but some never discover this. Some in this story are never healed. Why? Because the answers do not exist? No.

Because the characters neglect to connect.

When Jesus came to this earth, He was bold about His own scandalous history, and He was born under tabloid circumstances. Why? Simple.

Because He knew that His rough stuff was the answer to someone else's—and He did not want to keep it quiet. He knew that the only path to healing was to connect His glue to someone else's pieces.

In God's great plan He created us each the same way. We each have our own brokenness and we each have a God-given strength. However, we continue to sit in confusion because we feel like a life following Jesus should feel less disjointed and make more—well, sense.

And that is exactly the problem.

Our lives don't make sense because our lives were not intended to stand alone.

Our lives were each made by God as pieces. Pieces of the eternal puzzle.

We are made to fit our lives into one another's. Our *entire* lives. The good. The bad. The strength. And the rough stuff.

As hopeful as we are that our strength will heal someone else, it is far more likely that our rough stuff will. Because not only does our rough stuff hit another life where it most matters—the acknowledgment of our own rough stuff communicates that we understand this life we live and this world we live it in. Embracing the reality of our rough stuff communicates truth. Truth that the world is able to identify. Truth that will become the glue to their pieces.

This is the profound orchestration of how God intended to use imperfect people to represent a perfect God. God's intention was never for each of us to fake our way to an appearance of flawlessness. His intention was for each of us to become true and vulnerable in our pursuit of Christ while taking the glue of His power (even amidst the frailty of our humanness) to connect with the broken around us. It is this weave—this interlocked puzzle—this merging of shrapnel and adhesive into a beautiful picture—it is *this* that reveals the real truth of Jesus Christ. If we are ever to escape the Christian*ish*

and truly become little Christs, it will only be in this merging—
acknowledging that our strengths are from God and not our own,
while allowing that strength to mend the broken. But it does not
stop there. We also have to be willing to reveal our pieces so that
others' strengths can heal our own pain.

This is the perfect earthly picture of Christ. It requires a new sort
of church culture: a culture that no longer positions itself at the pret-
tiest angle, but rather gets down to the scandalous histories for the
sake of revealing to a world at large that Christ not only understands,
but can transform our pieces through the power of other broken
people.

Just like the rest of the world, my sons Jackson and Charlie fit
together. They are simultaneously each other's antithesis and each
other's antidote. Each other's miracle or each other's foil. It all depends
upon whether or not they are each willing to fit together and allow
the collision of their rough stuff and strength—their scandals and
successes—to make the sum of both entirely complete.

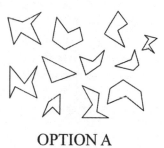

OPTION A   OPTION B

1. Can you relate to the flawed thinking that positioning and decorating ourselves—pretending the
rough stuff doesn't exist—ministers most?

2. Do you come from something scandalous? Do
you experience the rough stuff? Have you hidden
from this? Is that hiding drawing you closer to Christ
or driving a wedge between you? Is it drawing you
closer to others?

3. Consider the statement: *"We have done more
damage to the world's impression of Jesus by feigning inaccurate perfection than we could ever cause
by allowing those who don't follow Christ to see us
wrestling our sins and flaws to the ground."* Do you
agree or disagree? What are the detriments of hiding our struggle? What are the benefits of allowing
it to be seen?

4. Do you agree or disagree with the statement:
*"The lousy isn't rotten. The lousy isn't sin. The focus
of your life is not supposed to be dodging lousy.
Because lousy is life. And lousy is important"*? Why
or why not?

5. Have you considered your life "in pieces"? Have
you attempted to put yourself together on your
own?

6. What do you think of the philosophy that you are
actually a "piece"—that the solution to your life lies
in the way you fit together with the other people
who make up the community of this world?

wholiness 2

At the time, a second film in *The Cannonball Run* series seemed like the harbinger of good taste. I was young and excitable, and few films delivered the ribald hilarity and crash-'em-up high jinks of the Burt-Reynolds-races-hot-rods-illegally-across-the-heartland crowd-pleaser. It was the only movie from my childhood that intertwined comedy, car chases, martial arts, and Shirley MacLaine successfully. And that is really saying something.

The film was 108 minutes of ridiculousness featuring every celebrity of the era imaginable, from Jackie Chan and Marilu Henner to Tim Conway and Don Knotts to Sammy Davis Jr. and Frank Sinatra. And it was the worst film any of them ever made.

The largest problem with *Cannonball Run II* was that it did for my speeding urge what *Footloose* did for my desire to partake in gymnastics inside abandoned warehouses. The moment I walked out of that Saturday afternoon screening of the high-octane break-the-law-a-thon, I wanted to push my gas pedal to the floor and hear those tires squeal like the General Lee chasing moonshiners who just kidnapped Lulu Hogg. Fortunately, I was not quite fifteen years old, so even though I had a desire to speed, I had neither an automobile nor an opportunity.

This avoided truancy was a miracle in disguise. It turns out that my friend and I were not the only ones inspired by Burt Reynolds to put the pedal to the metal that day. As my friend drove me home from the movie, blaring the radio and rocking like a hurricane, we drove faster than we should. And then—just over the hill a quarter-mile up the road—we saw the incident—and gasped.

A Camaro came flying over the horizon.

It must have been topping out at over one hundred miles per hour. It was in the opposite lane, facing towards us, and it just flew—literally airborne—off the pavement. It careened out of control and then rolled, nose-over-nose, into a mangled and ghastly heap of metal. It was the most horrific car accident I had ever seen with my own eyes.

This was no movie.

We, along with every other witness, pulled over to the side of the road. Police cars appeared over the horizon within seconds, having clearly been chasing the perpetrator. Before we could break our stunned silence, officers surrounded the wreckage, motioning for us gawkers to stay away and drive home to the rest of our lives.

We climbed back into the car in complete silence and drove home.

At least ten miles an hour under the speed limit.

SIN SEEMING SENSIBLE

This is, of course, the nature of temptation. Not sin staring us in the face seeming *enticing*, but rather sin staring us in the face seeming *sensible.* After a screening filled with the carefree antics of Burt & Company, it seemed almost irrational to deprive ourselves of the elation that speeding would bring. Yes, technically it was against the law, but in the movie the police were imbeciles. The only policeman I would want to be friends with was Enos, and he always let Daisy Duke off with a smile and a warning. It never entered my mind that "everyone is doing it," but rather the distinct feeling that "everyone ought to try."

But sin only has a tendency to seem rational because it omits pertinent information. Sin grabs us with rational truth ("it will feel good") while discarding subsequent facts ("until it doesn't"). Sin has a great salesman: a voice that knows how to overmarket its menial, temporal benefits while downplaying the imbalanced cost.

We as a Christian*ish* culture are barely able to blink without giving in to temptation. Of course, we would vehemently battle this statement, because for the most part we believe we are dodging the biggies: sex, drugs, and non-Christian rock 'n' roll. But the idea that there are "biggies" at all (sins considered higher-level offense) is the most significant indicator that we have lost the plot.

As a church culture we don't tend to stumble obviously. This is what we chastise and shake our heads at. No, we only sin in public when it is acceptable to those who stare at us. We sin when it seems, well, sensible. When our greed to have the biggest church building in town overtakes any thought of the poverty-stricken in our community. When our yearning for bigger book sales causes us to skew more seeker-friendly than the message we know we are called to share. When our gifts shine and our ear is ever so slightly turned toward those who urge to us that we "have earned more" and "deserve better." When our anecdotes from the pulpit cease to be interesting enough—so we invent better ones.

It's the same as Burt Reynolds portraying the pleasures of speeding. It may seem simple and pleasant and safe—but it will lead to the same heap of mangled rubble in the end.

The truth is, we will be tempted. There is nothing we can do to stop it. The problem isn't really the temptation—nor is it merely the giving in to it. I mean, yes, giving in to temptation is a problem—but it isn't the largest problem facing the Christian*ish* in this arena. The largest problem is that we are so focused on what we deem the bigger temptations, that we are doing nothing at all about our response to the smaller ones. And it is these smaller temptations that eventually become devastating.

We wrap our accountability around lust and addiction: alcohol, drugs, sexuality, and the like. But we aren't very vigilant when it comes to materialism and excess. Pride and resentment. Rumormongering. Superiority and jealousy. Monitoring the words that come out of our mouths. Selfishness and greed. Negativism and divisiveness. In fact we do a pretty good job of ignoring that these all fester inside of us. Why? Because in modern society, they work. They move us forward. A broken society is electrified by broken efforts. Resisting the sins that seem sensible ties a knot in our otherwise smooth day. But it isn't the day that is at risk. It is what those days add up to.

I've known too many Christians whose faith and unaddressed sins sloshed against each other like nitro and glycerin. One day they inevitably exploded. When they did, the excuse was that their specific enormous sin issue was always a reality and they simply could not pretend anymore. Statements abound, such as, "this is like the thorn in Paul's flesh," or, "God made me this way, so I cannot change."

This is all, of course, hogwash.

We each have a sinful nature. We all have weaknesses that, unchecked, eventually become sin that can destroy our lives. But this dormant sin is not some fungus that will hatch no matter how deep our cleaning. It is a seedling that grows when we water and feed it, and we give sin sustenance when we excuse and bury the little stuff in our lives. Of course, no sin is little—but culture (and certainly the church) have minimized some while maximizing others, never acknowledging that the minimized, socially acceptable sins eventually do eternal damage.

In other words, the little things are what lead to the big. We give up early, stating the big things are unstoppable when in fact we haven't attempted to choke the little things.

We say we live in pursuit of holiness, but we only pursue it in the areas of our lives that our circle of community frowns upon. If those we esteem don't check our level of selfishness, then we don't see any need to put ourselves through the wringer. Because of this, we have developed a Christian*ish* culture that labels as "acceptable" many attitudes and approaches that are actually sin.

We bend the rules in business and finance, claiming that we are storing up the wealth of the wicked for the work of Christ. We manipulate others to do what we want by convincing them it's what Jesus wants, regardless of how much damage it may do to their marriage and family. We are experts at Jesus Blackmail. I have witnessed firsthand countless incidents when a ministry leader's inability to plan effectively turned into chaos for his team: continual nights and weekends away from a healthy life, getting a job done. The same goal could have been accomplished in a healthy manner, had the ministry leader been willing to effectively plan. Instead marriages crumbled and individuals turned away from ministry (and in some cases, Jesus) forever. The excuse given: Jesus deserves 100 percent. Well, yes He does. When are the ministry leaders going to give Him the sort of 100 percent that allows the people who work in their ministry to live out healthy and balanced lives? Not-so-fun-fact: If the people who work most closely with your ministry end up wanting nothing to do with Jesus, it is no longer a ministry. You have failed.

I've been a part of churches that developed a culture of personality, serving the individual pastor more sincerely and with more fervor than they serve Christ. As time passed, the quirks of each particular pastor's personality (brashness, insensitivity, coarse joking, bigotry, lack of kindness, passion for wealth) became the personality of the members of his congregation. And as sin has a tendency to stand out, the most negative quirk became the most prevalent characteristic of the church itself. The result: thousands led down a sin path and a pastor who eventually crashed and burned underneath the pressure of all that adulation. Meanwhile the world watched from the outside and had their suspicions confirmed once again: This church thing is all a big, fat lie.

The root of this comes from the age-old game called Scripture-plucking. When we first give our lives over to Jesus, we are altered by the realization of what the Word of God says, but the longer we live it out, the more we realize that we can take Scriptures out of context to defend just about every pattern of life that we want to justify. We play Russian roulette with the Scripture pages, finding a single anecdote that supports the theory we are most comfortable with. But the Bible was never created to defend *our* opinions. It was created to be meditated upon so that we would fully understand *God's* opinions. It is quite easy when we face temptation to go to the Word of God and attempt to explain our yearnings away with "Well, it is written …" It actually sounds fairly holy. We could even take the Scripture about God wanting to give us life more abundantly as an excuse to speed like Burt Reynolds. It's all in the interpretation. We think, "Hey. The Bible is holy, so quoting it must make my choices correct." But someone else tried that tactic before. Yeah. His name was Satan.

DOUBLE NEGATIVES

In Matthew chapter 4, Jesus was at a low point. He was in the wilderness and He was being tempted by the Devil (that's where these things tend to happen). The interesting predicament here is that this hellish forty-day window for Jesus was between two pinnacle moments in His life: the baptism—when God confirmed to all around that Jesus was indeed His Son—and the beginning of His ministry. There wasn't this *BOOM, BOOM: You're called, then it begins.* There was instead a *BOOM, BANG, BOOM: You're called, you go through the wringer, and then it begins.* (Why are we so flabbergasted when the same happens to us?)

Jesus had been fasting forty days and forty nights and He was very hungry. The Devil tried to mess with Him by playing with the idea of Jesus' authority: "If you are the Son of God, tell these stones to become bread." He used the old double negative. The "have you stopped beating your wife" line. There is no winnable answer. With that loaded question, Christ's next action would either cave in to Satan's request or attest to doubting He was the Son of God. Instead Christ took the third, unspoken option. He quoted Deuteronomy.

> *It is written: "Man does not live on bread alone, but*
> *on every word that comes from the mouth of God."*
>   Matthew 4:4

He didn't attempt to prove Himself externally of God's plan. He didn't need the ego boost. He didn't do something that appeared godly, He Himself being the only one who would've known that it really was not. Jesus had the wherewithal to make the right decision, even while starving and exhausted. Why? The reason is key: *Jesus knew that the two options the Enemy presented Him were not the only options.*

Why do so many ministries and individuals choose Christian*ish* paths? Because it is the better of what we perceive as the only choices in front of us. We excuse our ungodly behavior with thoughts like, *Well, this is just the way it is done* or *I live in a fallen world.* But the Christian*ish* options are never the only options. They are simply the only ones that seem to be immediately sensible. After all, we do tend to sacrifice eternal sense for immediate from time to time. In a time of crisis we will be presented with obvious options, but those options are oftentimes temporal. The only way we can also be familiar with the eternal options is if we are familiar with the Book of eternal options. We must become well versed in the verses of God. Not just some of the verses of God—ALL of the verses of God.

The Devil himself was familiar with *some* of God's verses. The second time he tempted Jesus in the wilderness, he threw the Book right back at Jesus. He thought to himself, "Okay, if you're going to use the Bible, so am I." Satan took Jesus to the holy city and had Him stand on the highest pinnacle. Satan said, "If you are the Son of God, throw yourself down, for it is written: 'He will command His angels concerning you, and they will lift you up in their hands, so that you will not strike your foot against a stone.'"

Wow. Satan quoted Psalm 91. The same Scripture that so many Christians quote as a wooden cross against the vampires of the world. It is a Scripture that tells us not to fear, because God will rescue us when we call out to Him. This moment in Matthew grips me, because Psalm 91 is the exact chapter in the Bible that I would have quoted (and actually *have* quoted) if I were in jeopardy. It would seem like the godly, rational thing to do. It freaks me out a little bit. In my human-ness, if I had been challenged in such a manner, with Satan saying, "If you believe your God is strong enough to save you, why don't you just jump," I would have felt an obligation to prove God accurate.

But that is not what Christ did.

Because Christ did not lean on a few choice Scriptures that supported His life perception. He leaned, instead, on *all* of them. He didn't just weigh the options Satan presented Him. He weighed the options that Satan *did not* present Him. This is where Jesus differs from us. He didn't consider the Enemy's word to be the complete picture. Instead He weighed all of God's options. Jesus spoke.

It is also written: "Do not put the Lord your God to the test."

Also written.

Also. This is the word we omit when we are tempted—and yes, we are tempted every day in more ways and in more moments than we would care to acknowledge. Every day we are starving in some spiritual area in our lives. It is in these moments that the enemy tempts us in what we would call the little things. He isn't brazen. He is sly. Like a *Cannonball Run* film, making the choice of the moment seem unimportant. Making the enticing sin seem like something we may just deserve.

In these moments, given the obvious choices in front of us, we will continue to take the unhealthy Christian*ish* path: the choice that doesn't offend those immediately around us, but nonetheless damages what Christ is trying to do in our lives. There is only one way we can be prepared to follow Christ instead. We must know what is *also* written. We must dig deeply into the whole truth.

For far too long the Christian church has been infected with the disease of using snippets of God's Word to defend our opinions. We have become a sound-bite religion. Choosing an opinion or a pulpit message first, then fortifying it with a quick look at our *Strong's Concordance*.

We must embrace the discipline of studying the Word of God and trying to fully understand the balance of everything Jesus had to say on a subject. We must understand context and subtext thoroughly, and not merely base our faith on which poetic lines serve our jones best. God's Word is not here to serve the servant. We the servants are here to serve God.

And believe me, we are in the wilderness.

We look at Scriptures such as Matthew 4 and we instantly claim, "When I am in the wilderness, I will do what Jesus did." But we ARE in the wilderness. Right now: this daily life on planet Earth where aspects of our spirit man starve and suffer from drought. We are smack-dab in the middle of our forty days and forty nights— but we don't realize it because we've gotten used to starving and we can't tell it's the Devil who is luring us into disobedience.

I am reminded of the angels who came to Sodom and Gomorrah to rescue Lot and his family. Those angels did their best to pull Lot's family away, but when the question was presented to Lot's sons-in-law, they didn't follow Lot because they assumed he was joking. Though God deemed them worthy of salvation, they were so accustomed to their world of temptation that they couldn't even see it was a world wicked enough to destroy.

Now I'm not condemning the people of the world. I love that God stuck us on this beautiful planet, and I love the people in it— even the ones who don't understand the truth about Jesus. I know I don't always act like I love them, but deep down, I do. This is exactly why I have got to get a radical grip on the whole truth of the Scriptures: the whole truth of Christ.

My current life pattern is evangelical Christianity's current pattern: to modify what I believe as culture changes—not modify my methods—but rather modify what I *believe*. Don't get me wrong. There is room for this, because I am human and you are human and the chance that everything we each believe about Jesus is 100 percent accurate is not very likely. But that isn't what I am talking about. I am talking about the fact that the more difficult it is to live up to what we know is God's truth, the more we *soften* that belief. We change it by making it weaker. We believe that this is making a faith in Christ more seeker-friendly, more attractive. We think it means we are being Jesus and loving the people of this world more.

Unfortunately it is actually the opposite.

Yes, the church is guilty of not separating the sin and sinner—of disregarding people and spreading hate because they didn't look like us or believe like we do. But the other extreme is no healthy expression of love either. We don't truly love mankind by becoming more like them. We truly love mankind by becoming more like Christ—and in turn revealing how they can become more like Christ. Christ is loving to all sinners—accepting of any man, woman, or child— regardless of what state of trouble or disobedience they are in. But at that point, Jesus loves them *toward* Himself. The direction toward Christ is indeed a direction away from sin. We cannot lead a world toward Christ and toward sin at the same time—no matter how small we deem that sin.

This is why, when Jesus was tempted in the wilderness the third time, He stopped debating. Instead He gave the Enemy the mandate:

"Away from me, Satan!"

This is the direct result of "it is *also* written." When we fully understand where God stands on an issue, our end result is that we want the temptation to be gone. We stop enjoying its company and instead discover a definitive approach to living like Jesus. An approach that makes clear, loving lines, while still holding fast to the absolute truth.

So what exactly is the truth that "it is also written" leads us to?

That every man sins.

Jesus hates sin, but Jesus loves every man.

If each man will allow it, Jesus will lead him away from sin.

So then the question arrives: How do we determine what is sin? Theologians have debated this issue for centuries, citing Scriptures that seem to contradict one another. Every human can find a scriptural thesis either supporting or condemning his own habits if he has the spare time. So how do we know for certain?

We know sin by what sin does.

The reality of sin is quite simple: Sin separates and sin destroys.

Sin separates us from God and from one another. Sin separates us from peace. Sin separates us from joy. Sin destroys stability, relationships, community. Sin forges a wedge of hatred between cultures, denominations, and political parties. Between interest groups, races, and genders. Sin convinces us that we are right and everyone else is wrong and that this distinction is more important than love. Sin numbs a heart until it no longer yearns after people—and eventually no longer after God.

It may not happen immediately, but eventually sin dissolves a human.

Regardless of how hard you attempt to defend your life habits, regardless of how acceptable they are in modern society or church community, if those habits accomplish any of the above, they are sin.

It hardly matters what you believe about your own behavior. It matters what your own behavior does to you. I was quite convinced when I walked out of *Cannonball Run II* that it was my God-given right to taste the freedom of 120 mph.

And then I saw that freedom crush a man to pulp.

I now see that I daily stand in the wilderness. I am daily prodded by the tempter.

The next time he comes my way, I want to know what is *also* written.

I will believe it.

I will live it.

And then I will be prepared to turn his direction and say,

Away from me.

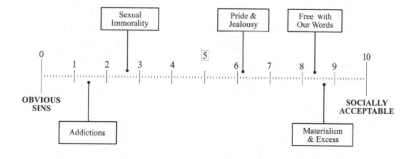

1. Do you find yourself focusing entirely on your "major" sin issues, or do you ever take the time for introspection to discover the sins in yourself that the church considers "minor"?

2. Are there sin issues that you do not address in your life because they make life in society "work better"? What are they?

3. Do you have any "I was born that way" sin issues? What do you think of the contrast between believing *sin is a fungus that spreads no matter what* and believing *sin is a seed that only flourishes when fed*?

4. Consider this statement: *"The little things are what lead to the big. We give up early, stating the big things are unstoppable when in fact we haven't yet attempted to choke the little things."* Have you found this to be accurate?

5. Have you ever been the victim (or the perpetrator) of Jesus Blackmail: manipulating others to do what one wants by convincing them it's what Jesus wants?

6. Are you guilty of Scripture-plucking: taking Scripture out of context to defend a pattern of life that you want to justify?

7. Consider this truth: *"Christ did not lean on a few choice Scriptures that supported His life perception. He leaned, instead, on all of them."* What would it require for this truth to become practical reality in your own life?

phariseesaw 3

For most people the size of their school tends to increase from kindergarten to high school. I guess I'm a bit backward in that regard. My elementary years were spent sharing space with about six hundred other kids at a Christian school in Columbus, Georgia. But a few years later, when my family moved to Atlanta, I settled into a downsized Christian schoolhouse of about two hundred and fifty kids. I would call it a country school, but it was on a main business throughway in Atlanta, Georgia. By the time I graduated from that school, it had become pretty tiny. When I say *tiny*, I'm not kidding. There were four people in my graduating class. Four. You couldn't even call that a home school. More like a homeless school. It spanned K through 12 and housed just shy of thirty students within that range. This made prom difficult. Heck, this made playing a Parker Brothers board game difficult.

Since that time I have worked with just about every Maxichurch and Uberministry you could imagine, but at the core I remain the small church boy from a humble community.

There were, of course, benefits to immersion in such a finite community. First off, I was the valedictorian—or as I like to call it: the top 25 percent of my class. Second, you couldn't help but be known by everyone exceedingly well. There was no room for fakery. If someone chose to serve Jesus with his or her life, it was obvious—and if someone chose not to—well, let's just say it's tough not to get caught smoking behind the storage barn when your body should otherwise be filling a fourth of the desks.

It was a lifestyle that didn't allow much in the way of privacy. If I had, hypothetically, slipped a Post-it note to the desk to my left, asking the brunette to "go with me" by checking a box, then everyone would know I had been turned down come lunch break. Even Jeremy, the stuttering first-grader, mocked me. I wasn't savvy with the girls on a historic level, but you really know your rep is scraping bedrock when the sarcastic pre-Ks are disdaining your courting habits.

My small school was a veritable petri dish of accountability. Not that you cared to know the goings-on of the other students on a truly intimate level, but you didn't really have a choice. If someone was smoking pot, you could smell it on their uniform across the room for days. If a girl was secretly pregnant, her tummy nudged the desk just enough to eliminate your legroom. There wasn't enough physical space to hide crushes, bruises, or tears. I couldn't even buy a Howard Jones cassette without it becoming an announcement in chapel.

However, this sort of knowing had one significant benefit. Within this level of proximity, if you had enemies, you were absolutely certain who they were. Enemies were, of course, few and far between. My lifetime enemies were limited to a few foils who were otherwise harmless:

- Sarah Pocklington, who attempted to seize many a kiss. I was six. I thought she was gross. She wasn't ugly. But I was six. She lived on the wealthy side of the golf course, and I would tag along with my dad every time he played nine holes instead of eighteen (this is, incidentally, how I learned the "s" word). Sarah would call out to me in that high-shrill voice: "Maaaark, come kiss me through the chain-link fence." My brother never let that one die. I wanted her incarcerated.

- Dino. I don't think he had a last name. I called him The Dino, with a capital T. He always knuckle-hit me in the arm and made fun of my pants. One time I wrote "Dino is my best friend" on the dedication page of my Bible. He wasn't. I hated him with the passion of a thousand white-hot gas balls, but I thought if he saw that I had written those words, the beatings would stop. He saw that I had written those words. The beatings got worse. I wanted him to fall into a pile of fire ants. A year ago I saw *Indiana Jones and the Kingdom of the Crystal Skull*. It was lame, but the villain fell into a pile of fire ants and they consumed him whole, beginning with his eyes and mouth. It was cool. I immediately thought of Dino.

- David G. I don't remember what the G stood for, but the girl I had liked forever liked him. He shaved his hair up on the sides and wore oversized paisley shirts buttoned to the top just like the guy in Scritti Politti. He was a suck-up, and his only talent was faking a coolish distance from all humanity. He used to abuse the girl I liked. I didn't know this until he was out of our lives. When I discovered this, I remember for a moment wanting him to die. I felt very guilty about that.

It probably isn't fair to call these people enemies. *Nemeses* is more to the point, but they were the closest reference I had whenever I turned to the New Testament and had the bile reach my Adam's apple as I read about the Pharisees. Those suckers just didn't get it, talking superior smack to the Savior, and I couldn't help but picture each of them wearing a man-nun-habit, the faces of Sarah and Dino and David G. poking through.

I was both startled and excited that Jesus' life had villains. Actual human beings who were so completely ignorant to His holiness that they became the melodramatic mwahaha caricature of Christian antagonism.

Pharisees were very handy come Sunday school. They created a necessary people-picture for Christians. A bit of a warning incarnate: *You see these dark-hooded, sinister, bearded, long-haired dudes on the flannelgraph board? Don't ever become like them.* To this end I established an unspoken definition of what a Pharisee must be. I knew that I loved Jesus and that the Pharisees betrayed Jesus. Therefore a Pharisee must be anyone who has betrayed me. Also—beards.

My first substantial betrayal came around the age of ten. It was a bus field trip to Callaway Gardens and I was seated next to the new kid because I had wanted to sit next to Tollie Ayscue, but Tollie had skipped breakfast and was currently spreading Vegemite onto a pita slice. The stench was palpable, so I scooted a few rows ahead and sat next to the only dude on the bus who was partnerless.

Harold.

Harold had enrolled at the beginning of the year, but the circles of camaraderie had been established the year prior. I had hardly noticed him even attempting to merge himself into one of the closed circles. My group—consisting of Tollie, David Reardon, Alan Blood, and me—was the elite group in the fourth grade. This was only partly because our leader's name was Blood. More accurate was the fact that we often opened the exterior power transformer that ran the phone lines and stripped the wires out of it. This made us seem dangerous, when in reality the wires were colorful and we liked to twist them into friendship rings.

David and Alan were inseparable, so I often sidled by Tollie, with whom I had the least in common.

On this particular day, we were driving a very long distance in order to hop off our bus and onto a tram that would drive us around the Gardens. A nature carpool. I vaguely remember a lengthy tour narration over the speaker system while only 11 percent of the animals and flora mentioned in the prerecorded commentary actually appeared out the windows.

The entire time, I sat beside Harold. It began awkwardly at best. I was never much of a chit-chatter, unless a parent or authority necessitated it. If I was asked to befriend someone, I could literally chatter for hours while chit flowed out of my mouth.

This was the case with Harold. My mother was not with me, but I knew from past experience that if I was ever stranded next to a person who had no friend, I was to become that friend. It was a mandate. This is why I detest sitting next to strangers on an airplane. If the flight has ended and I have not yet been named a legal guardian over future offspring, I feel guilty.

I was not all that comfortable with silence as a child because it seemed like it was a vacuum where a punch line should have existed. To this end I began throwing random comments out to Harold in hopes that it would at least alleviate the awkwardness of waiting for the prerecorded woman on the intercom to describe a nonexistent peony.

ME: *So did you move to Georgia over the summer or did*
           you just get expelled from a public school?
                    Are your parents divorced? Mine don't believe
           you can be a Christian and be divorced. Same thing
           with drinking and watching Bewitched.
                    The way that shrub is cut makes it look like the
           face of Gopher on The Love Boat.
                    I crammed about forty-seven Jolly Ranchers in
           my lunchbox. I put my bologna sandwich in the
           plastic sleeve of my denim notebook to make room. I
           like it better when the mayonnaise is warm anyway.

And that is when I saw Harold's lunch box. *The Dukes of Hazzard.* Not just any Dukes of Hazzard lunch box. *The* Dukes of Hazzard lunch box. The one with the faces of Bo and Luke on one side with the General Lee midair, while on the other side, the entire family (including Daisy) leaned against the hood. Orange trim. Black metal handle to match the numbers on the side of the car. The thermos had Boss Hogg and Rosco in the background with a big face of Enos. It was the best lunch box in the whole universe. It was the one I had wanted when I first saw it at the Family Mart, but by the time we went shopping, the wealthy kids had picked them off.

You must first understand that this was in a season of my life when the Duke Boys were 87 percent of what I lived for. Every Friday evening at eight o'clock, Waylon Jennings would sing the theme song and then we would watch the inhabitants of Hazzard County outrace drug smugglers and jewel thieves. Hazzard County was, of course, not real—but due to the fact that it was supposed to be in Georgia, we could not help but have a sense of ownership in the franchise. I looked down at Harold's lunch and simply muttered,

ME: *Dukes?*

It was enough to finally garner Harold's attention. He glanced up.

ME: *You like the Duke Boys?*

Harold did indeed like the Duke Boys. In fact he stated that he knew John Schneider and Tom Wopat personally and that they filmed the show in the woods behind his house.

ME: *What?! Freaking WHAT?!*

I could not believe my fourth-grade ears. Here I had not even wanted to sit next to Harold, and NOW I was making a discovery akin to the Holy Grail or the whereabouts of fire ants that could consume my enemies whole. It seemed completely insane. What were the chances that some dude I stumbled upon would be the key to my lifelong (okay, two-year) dream of *meeting* the Duke Boys? And yet, it was happening. Undeniably *happening!* It had to be true, or why would

Harold say it? I mean, who could possibly even dream up a story like that if it weren't true?

ME:	*Say that again.*
HAROLD:	They make the TV show *The Dukes of Hazzard* in the woods behind my house.
ME:	*With the actors and everything?*
HAROLD:	Uh-huh.
ME:	*And Boss Hogg?*
HAROLD:	Yep.
ME:	*And the General Lee?*
HAROLD:	You know it.

I paused for the moment of anticipation.

ME:	*And Daisy?*
HAROLD:	AND Daisy.

So Harold and I rapidly became best friends. I ditched Tollie, Alan, David, and their stupid illegal phone-cord friendship rings. I instead spent my breaks and lunches strategizing the opening conversation with Schneider and Wopat when we would finally meet. I would begin with trivia. Little-known minutiae that I had absorbed regarding the show and its extended mythology that I had mostly invented myself on a notebook I hid in my drawer under my stack of *Dynamite* magazines. Then the conversation would transition toward their other works. I was fairly certain Mom had mentioned Uncle Jesse had been on *Andy Griffith*. And what was that one movie John

Schneider did about the escaped convict? *Eddie Macon's Run!* Yes—I
would definitely lead with that. Of course, the inevitable conclusion
of the conversation would be when John and Tom asked me to costar
in an episode. If they asked, I had a two-page treatment handy.

Counting the days to this life-altering meeting was excruciating.
Harold could not take me to the area where they shot the episodes
until I spent the night with him because he lived almost an hour away.
My parents had a strict policy of needing to know my friends' parents
before I could spend the night at their house. This seemed insane to
me. What could possibly happen overnight at a stranger's house in
the woods an hour away from home? Talk about overprotective.

But after six months my parents finally conceded, feeling they
knew Harold's parents enough to allow me to sleep over. I was in
utter euphoria, staring at the school clock as the minutes ticked away.
Not that I needed to stare at the minutes. You could calculate passing
time in Mrs. Brooks's class by the fifteen-minute intervals between
Tollie's Vegemite farts.

And then the evening came. I rode home with Harold and his
mother. An hour had never felt so long. It didn't feel like a *Dukes of
Hazzard* hour. It felt more like a *Waltons* hour. Ugh. When we arrived
at the home, I knew I had to play things cool. We couldn't just jump
right into the excitement. Spending the night at a new friend's house
required a certain order of decorum: First, there was the reviewing of
the room, being introduced to the corners and projects that made it
unique—*Hey. I have that same* Greatest American Hero *poster. Didn't
know they made two of those.* Second, there was small talk with the
mom over a snack. The snack in question established a large amount
of information. If the mother freely wielded Ho Hos or Cheetos,

you knew you were in the friend zone. Carrots and Vegemite? Well, that's what we call a school-hours-only pal. Harold's mom offered up Twinkies, Coke, and Pixy Stix. Man, oh man. And then—and only when the mom said, *Why don't you boys go play outside*—could the adventure begin.

Harold ran through the woods and I chased after him, anxious to stumble upon what would certainly be hundreds of people with cameras, and then—over a forthcoming hill—I could practically taste the inevitable sight of it: the General Lee being scrubbed down by Catherine Bach in a tied-up sleeveless button-down.

HAROLD: It's just over here!

Harold shouted and I followed over the hill. There, on the other side—was a creek bed.

ME: *What's this?*
HAROLD: Creek bed. It's awesome. I play here all the time.
ME: *When do we see where they shoot Dukes of Hazzard?*
HAROLD: What? Dude—I made that up.
ME: *You—you—you—you—*
HAROLD: Mark, are you okay?
ME: *You what?!*
HAROLD: I was just joking around. You didn't really believe
            me, did you?

And I had. I had completely believed him. Surrendered my faith and trust to what my emotions wanted to be true, and therefore

bought into 100 percent. In fact my entire friendship with Harold
had been rooted in this single charade. I had idolized the Duke
Boys and I wanted to meet the Duke Boys. Harold was merely the
stool I would have stepped on to become tall enough to shake their
hands. I was crushed. Utterly mortified. Which is why my answer
to Harold was ...

ME: *Of course not.*

Our friendship went on for years, but all along the path I kept
a suspicious internal distance, surmising that anything good coming
out of Harold's mouth might just be inaccurate. In the meantime,
however, I never took a single notice of my own hypocrisy in the
proceedings.

True, Harold had drawn me into the friendship on false pre-
tenses—something I certainly deemed betrayal at the time—but I
had entered the friendship just as fraudulently. I had been hesitant at
best, only gung-ho when the friendship suddenly became an e-ticket:
an opportunity for me to get a bonus beyond the actual relationship
itself.

CHRISTIANITY-MAXIMIZERS

It dawns on me now that *this* is actually the definition of the Pharisees
I saw as my nemeses. Not that they are Christian-haters, but rather
that they are Christianity-maximizers. Individuals who use a pursuit
of Christ for their own personal gain rather than for the life-giving
relationship that it is intended to be.

Certainly I had always realized a portion of this. Of course, I had only realized it in relation to acknowledging the flaw in others. I saw other people's hypocrisy while never applying the Pharisee definition to myself. My old Sunday school definition and this new discovery simply swayed back and forth on the teeter-totter of my mind, favoring whichever definition worked best for me in a given situation. And now the old Sunday-school flannelgraph has jumped off its end of the Phariseesaw, causing reality to throw my derriere to the dirt of the playground floor.

Of course, we all know that Jesus is love. But that didn't stop Him from having sharp words for His nemeses. We picture Him wordless, overturning tables in His rage, letting the trashing of the fellowship hall speak for itself, when in reality the words of His very first recorded sermon set the bar high for how He would respond to humanity. It was a diatribe flip-flopping the hierarchy of the day, announcing that what the church of the time was saying it meant to follow God was actually a path away from Him. His words were crystal clear. There was no clouded parable, no cryptic symbolism— instead a straightforward announcement that the world had better upside-down itself fast.

The message was called the Beatitudes, and though we praise it in modern Christianity, we don't seem to be paying very close attention to its ideology. Either that or we are being very loose in defining words, where Jesus was extremely direct. The thinking of the day was that affluence and influence insinuated an individual was more blessed of God. The Pharisees were seen as the holiest because they knew the most and owned the most—a sentiment that resounds even more loudly in the modern church.

Jesus blew a maelstrom through that line of thinking with the very first words out of His mouth in the very first recorded sermon He gave:

Blessed are the poor in spirit, for theirs is the kingdom of heaven.

Excuse me, *what* now? In a world where not only did the Pharisees believe they were holier—*but everyone else believed they were as well*—this thought was like installing a sliding-glass door in solitary confinement.

Now, just like any passage in Scripture, we in the church tend to make of this statement whatever we want it to mean. We say it refers to the humble, or to those who have much but give the credit freely to God (i.e., they are loaded in "life," but poor in "spirit." Honorary poverty. Spiritually slumming). We say it refers to those who have given up much willingly for God. And in some ways it may just mean a little bit of all of those things. But what it certainly means as well is that those who are downtrodden—at the very end of who they are, beat up and given up—theirs is the kingdom of heaven. Not only that they might just receive the crumbs, but that it is *primarily* theirs. Why?

Because Jesus is looking for people who are at the end of themselves.

We've all reached this point on some level, but due to the modern church's take on the matter, we assume the end of ourselves is a punishment for sin. That it is just deserts for all the bad choices in our lives. That God has ripped every good thing away from us to make us wish we had never crossed Him. But the opposite is actually true.

It is *only* at the end of ourselves that we can truly surrender the need to comprehend what the bonus of faith will deliver for us. Most of us live our faith at the top of ourselves. In this state, though we may not intend or realize it, we play church for the sake of what we can milk out of its teat. We are in it for compensation. Not necessarily for the opportunity to have a televised ride-along in the General Lee, but for something, nonetheless. That compensation may be emotional or enlightenment, or it may be esteem and a place in a community. Either way, our path of righteousness is steeped in a yearning for even more stuff. But that doesn't happen at the end of ourselves. At the end of ourselves, when we find that we have nothing left but God's grace, a funny thing happens.

We stop wanting more than God's grace.

We suddenly uncover the reality that His grace is not only enough stuff, but it is actually the only stuff that really matters. And when God's grace becomes the only thing that matters in our perspective, all other stuff falls into its proper place. Christian relationships become richer and more selfless. Our efforts within a church structure become valuable and life-giving internally and externally. Because those efforts stop being the stuff.

It's easy to live faith at the "top" of ourselves. Heck, the Pharisees lived at the top of themselves: the place where we are esteemed for what we seem to be. A lot of people at the top of themselves have a legitimate faith in God. The problem is that it sits even-steven on the teeter-totter with their faith in themselves. That's what Jesus came to knock off.

To this end Jesus moved forward rapidly with His sermon, continually reiterating what it means to be at your very end:

Blessed are those who mourn ...
The meek ...
Those who hunger and thirst for righteousness ...
The merciful ...
The pure in heart ...
The peacemakers ...
Those who are persecuted because of righteousness.

He pretty much eliminated all of our organized, elitist efforts right there. We don't tend to pursue these places with a whole lot of fervor. Who wants to be at the end of yourself when you can have a pulpit and a three-book deal? Who wants to mourn? Even if we are in a place of mourning, everything inside of us tells us not to openly show it. We certainly don't spend much of our church currency on urging one another to be meek, merciful, or peacemaking. Meek? Are you kidding? Blessed are those who get walked on? Blessed are those who don't play the get-ahead game? We thought we corrected all that thinking in the eighties.

THE ACCEPTABLE ADDICTION

And yet Jesus went there. He made it clear that if we want to inherit the earth, we have to eradicate our need to be seen as correct. But this is the modern church's acceptable addiction. Not only that Christ be seen as the Way, but rather that our personal approach be seen as the way to the Way. We fight within denominations and between variations of nondenominations. We speak out against other ways more than providing a clear way ourselves. We promote -*isms* and endorse candidates and decry interest groups. We lambaste and insult and boycott and do very little in the way of developing meekness. And of course, we defend loudly that the reason we do so is because Jesus is correct and Jesus deserves to be acknowledged as correct. In so doing, we miss the point of meekness altogether. Jesus *is* correct. But it is not our role to vehemently argue that fact. It is our role to *lead people to Jesus*. Only Jesus can draw men's hearts and minds to Him. A part of His correctness—His Godness—is that this works when we merely lead people to Him in ways where their ears and eyes are ready to truly listen and look. Instead we harden hearts to His correctness by our methods. We are a loudspeaker and we think we are amplifying "Jesus is right," but all we are magnifying is the sentiment "*we* are right" and the feedback we are creating is drowning out the truth.

The truth is, modern Christianity in action has had very little to do with this list. Jesus acknowledged the poor in spirit first, marking its significance. Yet most of our modern efforts make great attempts to pretend that such a thing does not even exist in the church. We don't want people to think that a follower of Jesus could possibly be poor in spirit, because that seems weak. It seems like a loser who has allowed the unchurched of the world to win. And if modern political-socio-religion has taught us anything, it is that serving Christ is about *winning*. About being on the right team.

But Christ didn't split the world into teams. He actually created a single family. And He yearns every moment for the millions of prodigal sons and daughters. So much so, that when one finally comes to Him, His first response is grace. Meekness and grace. Yes, there will be an addressing of the ways they live that are not pleasing to God, but He doesn't open with that. He leads with outstretched arms—and He expects us to do the same.

We don't.

Instead we play the faithful older brother, perturbed that our runaway sibling is getting the same or better treatment as we are, though we woke up for the early service and baked the freaking cake the runaway is now having for breakfast.

Looks like that older brother would have gotten along very well with the Pharisees.

Of course, we get excited about the results offered up in the Beatitudes. We can hardly wait to receive what's on the tail end of our efforts:

> ... *theirs is the kingdom of heaven.*
> ... *they will be comforted.*
> ... *they will inherit the earth.*
> ... *they will be filled.*
> ... *they will be shown mercy.*
> ... *they will see God.*
> ... *they will be called sons of God.*

You would be hard-pressed to find an American church service where the reading of those deliverables does not drum up a hearty supply of amens. But are we really paying attention to the cost? We see these results and we are quick to determine by the outcome that the first half of each sentence must already apply to our lives.

Those who mourn? Yes. I am sad for the less fortunate. I just mailed them a sweater that no longer fits me.

The meek? Certainly I don't say every critical thing that comes to mind.

Those who hunger and thirst after righteousness? Oh, yes. I want everything that God has and I want everyone to know that I want it.

The merciful? The pure in heart? The peacemakers? Well—it's good to have goals.

Persecuted because of righteousness? That's referring to Old Testament times, right?

And on and on, yearning for the bonus but dodging the finger pointed at my own chest. I've read this passage in Matthew chapter 5 literally a hundred times. It is now time to truly dwell on what it requires of me. To read this passage—not from the vantage point of "how might that be describing me already"—but instead with the intent of rooting out where I am the Pharisee in question.

Perhaps, in many ways, I have been Jesus' nemesis while calling Him my friend. I have been the older brother ticked about the feast being stuffed into the forgiven one's mouth. I have been the Pharisee tsk-tsking those who don't do things my/God's way. Not serving Jesus, but rather standing on His back to reach the high cookie jar so that I can serve myself.

And the thud of this realization becomes crystal clear when I read the last statement in the Beatitudes.

> *Blessed are you when people insult you, persecute you*
> *and falsely say all kinds of evil against you because of*

me. Rejoice and be glad, because great is your reward
in heaven, for in the same way they persecuted the
prophets who were before you.

Matthew 5:11–12

The truth is, there's not a whole lot of evil being said against me these days because of Jesus. And why would there be? I've been making a name for myself instead of Him. I've been covering my own butt by establishing my own correctness. In the midst, most who observe me think I'm on the right track without righteousness playing a role whatsoever. It's not that I wasn't interested in righteousness, but I certainly didn't hunger and thirst after it, now did I? I didn't crave it or starve for it.

Instead I craved something else altogether. Not righteousness, but instead accurateness. I-told-you-so-ness. And in the pursuit of this state, I didn't risk being persecuted for Christ's sake at all.

In fact I spent an awful lot of time accepting praise for things Jesus did while giving Him the negative rap for my own mistakes. The result? People thought highly of me, but when they saw me fail, they thought negatively of God. How backward is that?

It is exactly why we as a church body must come to the end of ourselves. Not merely to experience the fullness of His grace, but so that the prodigals of the world can witness the fullness of His grace and realize it is there for them as well.

No, this won't result in each of us looking like we are winning.

But it might go a long way in eradicating the need for teams.

CHRISTIAN-   **CHRISTIANITY-**
HATERS   **MAXIMIZERS**

1. Consider this definition of a Pharisee: *"Not Christian-haters, but rather Christianity-maximizers: individuals who use a pursuit of Christ for their own personal gain rather than for the life-giving relationship that it is intended to be."* Do you agree or disagree? Why?

2. Do you agree that the kingdom of heaven is primarily for those who have reached the end of themselves? What does the end of yourself look like?

3. Do you find that your Christianity is steeped only in the pursuit of God's grace—or do you inadvertently seek other compensation? Be introspective for a moment. What is this compensation? What have you been living to get out of church and faith?

4. If grace is the only stuff that matters, what does that say about all the other legitimate needs that we have been striving to fulfill through faith?

5. Think through the Beatitude list: the poor in spirit, those who mourn, the meek, those who hunger and thirst for righteousness, the merciful, the pure in heart, the peacemakers, those who are persecuted because of righteousness. Does this list reflect your life? The life of your church community?

6. Are you known more for what you are for, or are you known more for what you are against?

7. Do you believe serving Christ is about winning? If not, what is it about?

shut up already 4

I have a love-hate relationship with the microphone. Yes, I am grateful for the times it has amplified my attempts at wit, allowing it to bounce off an audience and return with love. But I am equally mortified by the number of times I have been backstage and forgotten the blasted thing was on. This does in fact mean that my efforts in the bathroom were amplified—but it also means upon occasion I whispered words for no one else's ears, forgetting that the audio man was paying close attention.

Trust me. Do not tick off the audio man. He may not be able to control the actual words you say, but he plays a significant role in how those words are perceived by everyone else. And of course, he is always listening.

I can't actually blame the microphone itself, because my lips, teeth, and tongue have gotten me into more substantial trouble in my life than any other combination of body parts.

There have been a significant number of instances when my oth-erwise kindhearted nature was thwarted irrevocably by my tongue's need to spitfire a punch line. It simply could not be helped. Let's face it, when my fellow second-grader sitting beside me said something like *I'm glad Kermit is the smartest puppet,* my lips would begin to tremble and form the retort before I could stop them. My Sunday school teacher would give me the rigmarole about self-control and the mouth being Satan's waterslide, but I had no choice. If I were to hold in all my comments about the irrationality of Jim Henson's hand having more intelligence than Frank Oz's, my eyes would melt. One-liners poured into my brain about the innate acumen of lime green felt as opposed to pink. Of the increased proclivity toward a higher Mensa score for candidates with googly eyes. The mind is not meant to suffer such taming. And don't even get me started about calling Kermit a *puppet.* This was akin to heresy. The fusillade of comebacks would pour out of my mouth like a nicotine exhale. I would insult. I would demean. And I would be at peace.

The school I attended had a disciplinary structure based on warnings, demerits, and detentions. If misbehavior was established, there would be a verbal warning. A third warning earned a demerit and a third demerit warranted a detention. A detention meant staying after school, while three detentions in one week earned a paddling. A paddling was what they called a spanking for people over the age of seven. I don't know why three was the magic number for each increase in punishment, but it had little to do with Scripture and a lot to do with the rules of baseball. I believe a third paddling equaled the forever surrendering of one's left arm or leg. Personally I avoided the detention, because I was required to have documents signed by a parent or guardian and, as I was unable to convince the lady who sold us Now and Laters at the Tenneco that she could be considered my guardian, this could only mean my father.

However, since three warnings equaled a demerit and three demerits equaled a detention, this meant that I could get a full eight punch lines in throughout a single school day before it would turn into punishment my dad had to sign off. For someone with my proclivities, this was not such a healthy realization.

To this end I had an irritating verbal witticism for everything (or at least the first eight everythings of each school day). This made me an anomaly of a young man. Everyone wanted to be my friend at the top of the day, but by the 10:15 first break, they remembered why they stopped liking me yesterday. But I didn't care—because I felt like my jokes made me better somehow: smarter and more anecdotal, like Mark Twain, David Addison, or Bullwinkle.

RAMIFICATIONS

But as much as my sarcastic and comedic words got me into trouble, they paled in comparison to the real culprit: *braggadocio*. This is an Italian word for pompous jerk. Italian words always sound better because they allow you to picture the heinous concept in question with a side order of breadsticks.

I wasn't good at many things, but when I was, I overcompensated with ego. This resulted in thudding ramifications at the age of thirteen (they call them ramifications because they head-butt you off the edge of the Alps) when I joined a few dozen students my age on a bus excursion toward the Tri-State Christian School Regional Competition.

If you've never been a part of a Christian school or, better yet, never joined a slew of other Christian students on a trip to a regional competition, you're missing out. And by "missing out," I mean "keeping your belief system intact." The Tri-State Christian School Regional Competition was made up of schools from five states (defining "tri-" was clearly not an educational aspect of the competition), which would come together at a summer-camp facility for the sole purpose of academic smackdown, proving that, though we all serve the same God, some of us serve him with more awards.

In the daytime we would go head-to-head with other uniform-wearing schools in contests of academia and theology. Yes, theology. There was a preaching category (won this particular year by a young Baptist named Donnie whose sermon was entitled "Sin Is Sinful." He scored a ninety-nine, being deducted one point for capitalizing "sinful"). There were also contests between the girls that we could only call "The Future Pastor's Wife Challenge." This was a musical toe-to-toe between ingenues in matching Dolly Parton hairstyles, each singing a sixty-second spiritual standard to a pipe organ accompanist. Our understanding was that the piano was a no-no because you had to tap your foot a little in order to play. An instrumental track was frowned upon as well because the cassette was inserted into the player the same way an AC/DC tape might be. Our friend entered with a little ditty called "I've Found It and You Can Find It Too (I've Found New Life in Jesus)." Yes, it's a verbose title, but if one were to remove the parenthetical sub-line, the song would suddenly become secular: *Exactly what has been found that is being offered to others? Peyote? Fornication? A Wham! song? And what's with all this looking and finding? Sounds exhausting.*

She lost.

It was the evenings, however, when the young seized a vestige of youth. All of the guardians and judges would fall asleep by 6:15, and this would officially begin the reign of terror. Each and every student had brought an extra suitcase filled with shaving-cream cans, pocket-knives, and enormous doses of caffeine. To make matters worse, the camp's general store sold thin strands of leather. These were intended to aid in one of the craft categories. It had not been foreseen that most of the thirteen-year-old boys would buy up the lot, fashion them into leather whips, and then battle one another senseless.

This particular trip, I was new to the school so I had not entered many categories. This allowed for a great deal of wandering around in between my events. It is also how I discovered Academic Bowl.

When I initially saw this event on the sign-up sheet, I dodged it, assuming the term "bowl" insinuated a need for athletic prowess. It was fairly clear by the body types walking into the geodesic dome that this was not the case.

I entered and sat near a table of four of my schoolmates. They were seated neatly in a row, dressed to the nines, and leaning confidently on their folding poker table. (I hoped the judges never found out what those tables were used for, or we would be required to compete leaning only on our own laps.) There was a small ding-bell in the middle of the table. The rules became clear: A Christian-academic category would be named from the following options:

- *Advanced Mathematics Based on Measurements of the Tabernacle*

- *Creationism vs. Anti-Creationism*
- *How Short Was Jesus' Hair?*
- *Old Testament Lineages*
- *Solomon's Use of Sex as a Symbol for Abstinence*
- *Pre-Babel Spelling*
- *Native Americans & Other Sinners*

A question would be read from each category. As soon as the conundrum was proposed, whoever dinged the bell first won the option to venture an answer. Correct answers were three points each (again with the three!). At the end of a round of forty-nine questions (seven times seven), one school would be named the most anointed in the arena of academia.

I could barely contain my euphoria. A contest measuring know-it-allness?! That was my specialty. My calling. Correct answers? I can do that. Superiority? You got it. Timely bell-dinging? I could totally learn.

But I had not signed up for Academic Bowl. So I would be required to sit quietly and observe.

Observe, I did.

Quietly, not so much.

For the next ninety minutes, every time a question was posed, before anyone could answer, I would GASP!

Seriously. I would literally expel an audible *OHP!* and clasp my hand over my mouth, sometimes inserting my entire fist in to tame myself from blurting out my elite brainsmanship. It was extremely awkward. Between the perceptible *WHOA! BOOP!* of my reined-in comments and the flailing of my appendages as they admirably kept my mouth from proving all other contestants mentally stunted, I had very few friends in that auditorium.

Several times the emcee actually halted the contest, standing three inches away from me (again with the three) and stating (supposedly to the entire room, but with his hand on my shoulder),

We politely remind the audience to keep absolutely silent and still throughout the remainder of the competition. Absolutely. Silent. And. Still.

He then gave me the Headmaster Glare. You know. The glare that says, "I can make your young Christian life a living hell. Also, I can have your pet killed."

From that moment on I shut up. I did, however, corner our school's team captain, Steve, after their drubbing of a loss.

ME: *Dude! I cannot believe you didn't know those answers! You're totally the headmaster's son and you did NOT know the answers. I knew ALL of those answers!*

STEVE: Really. No kidding.

ME: *Like when they asked how many years did Methuselah live and you said around 970 and I'm thinking Dude! It's 969. It's 969 EXACTLY! Like in that song on "Bullfrogs & Butterflies"!*

STEVE: Must have missed that one.

ME: *PLUS, King Xerxes has two Xs—and there's not an O at all. What you spelled means to photocopy something.*

STEVE: Please leave.

ME: *And a TISHBITE! Fool! Elijah was a TISHBITE!*
           You spend waaaaay too much time playing
           basketball.

STEVE: I'm walking away now.

ME: *And ANYTHING with a dinosaur is a TRICK*
           QUESTION. Bro—YOU KNOW THAT!!

A subtle wedge was being formed in our friendship, which made no sense to me because all I was doing was reiterating where he was stupid and I was superior. Isn't that called accountability?

The next day, the second round of the Academic Bowl took place, and the moment I walked through the door, you could hear the entire audience filling the room with an "Ughhhh." The moderator walked over to me preemptively and reminded me that it was necessary to keep quiet throughout the proceedings. I felt that he must be speaking to someone behind me, because I had not considered my gasps and moanings to be actual noise. It began to slowly dawn on me that I was being rejected.

WHAT?! Rejected? For massively heightened intellect? I am being penalized simply because my schoolmates see me as a tangible reminder of their own ignorance. Who needs these weirdos? I left the proceedings, partly because they were boring without my involvement, but mostly because everyone had stopped looking at me.

After a very quiet and lonely bus ride back to Georgia, we arrived at the school by midday. It was quickly announced that a special assembly was going to be held to finish off the afternoon and welcome the competitors home. The meat of this assembly would be a Mock

Academic Bowl, pitting the school's official team against a group of four other students selected at random. It was swiftly brought to my attention that I was one of the random students selected! I could hardly believe the collision of coincidence that was making this opportunity possible. It was almost as if it had been planned.

As we were seated in front of the remainder of the school, my seat to the immediate right of our ding-bell, I glanced over at the other team only to see all four of them smiling snidely in my direction. My stomach began to sink. Certainly they bore no ill will to me for my behavior out of town. After all, I had only played the microphone to their public failings. The questions began to hit fast and furious:

1. *What is the hypotenuse of the triune God?*
2. *Spell "Maher-shalal-hash-baz."*
3. *Explain the scientific improbability of the ax head floating on the water and elaborate on how it distracts attention away from the real point of the chapter.*
4. *Wrestle a Nephilim to the floor—describe your soreness in essay form.*
5. *Build Noah's ark out of construction paper using actual biblical measurements to scale. Please waterproof materials.*
6. *Debunk another major religion in less than thirty words.*
7. *Make a local mountain move four inches with only faith and a mini-crowbar.*

Hey.

These weren't the same questions they had on the trip. These were difficult. A tall order. I began to feel small streams of sweat trickle across my hairline and then down into my ear. I began to be preoccupied with the uncomfortable sensation of sweat in my ear and therefore forgot to ding the bell on the occasional question I did know. I was losing credibility and losing it quickly. I needed to answer a question FAST.

8.   *What is the text of the 177th verse of Psalm 119?*

DING! I blurted out—

> *"I have strayed like a lost sheep. Seek your servant, for I have not forgotten your commands"*!

There was an eruption of laughter. OF COURSE! There is no 177th verse of Psalm 119! Everyone knows it stops at verse 176. Everyone.

My random team lost the contest irrevocably. It wasn't even remotely close. As school dismissed for the day, I began to gather my books for the long walk through my gathered schoolmates to my mom's car. As I was just about to walk away from the table with the ding-bell, the school headmaster looked my way with a glance that distinctly read "that's what you get for being a know-it-all."

Hold on just a second.

It dawned on me that this entire ruse had been planned. I had not been chosen randomly. These questions were not unintentionally impossible for me to answer. I had been set up to be made the fool in front of my entire social circle. My indignation rose as I realized that I had done absolutely nothing to deserve this. Well—nothing except for making the headmaster's son look like a fool in front of every school leader in the district. *Ohp.* Perhaps that wasn't the wisest step forward in the relationship.

My mouth had done irreparable damage yet again. In my attempt to seem witty and wise and correct, I had alienated friends and established brand-new nemeses. Yes, my intelligence was accurate, but the method in which I had thrust that accuracy upon others made them resent both the truth and me. To this end their bile had been so stirred up by my approach, they had actually taken the time to devise my public downfall.

I never spoke of any of these incidents again. I never explained to my parents what had occurred at school and how mortified I had been. I certainly never clarified what I had done out of town to deserve it. A few weeks later summer began—and when we returned back to school in the fall, that same headmaster had abandoned our school and taken 80 percent of the families with him to start a new school of his own. This is how my school became less than thirty people. This is also how my arrogance had remained secret.

BETTER-THAN

But while my arrogance remained secret, in the modern church our arrogance is no secret at all. It is so brazenly and openly declared that it is stunting the reception to the truth that we tell. We have been putting forth Christian thoughts with decidedly Christian*ish* methods that turn the unchurched world off to any life-giving realities we might be purporting. In other words, our ideology might be heavenly, but our methods of communicating it border on hellish.

We have embraced the philosophy of *better-than*: Once we discover the life-changing truth of Jesus Christ, we are somehow superior to everyone else. We may not feel this or think we believe this, but our methodology reeks of it. We are quick to turn God's righteousness into our own, using it as a launchpad for our politics and opinions, even if those opinions do not line up with Scripture. The sad truth is that each and every one of us is human, and once we choose to follow Jesus with our life, we continue to be human. We continue to have flaws in our thinking and behavior, even flaws that we believe to be sacred truth. But none of us has the capacity as human beings to be 100 percent accurate in our understanding of who God is completely. He is beyond all we could ask, think, or imagine. To this end our individual perceptions of Him have zero chance of being entirely sound. In other words, just because a Christian feels something passionately does not make it God's way. Just because a pastor preaches it from the pulpit does not make it God's take on the matter. Just because an entire modern Christian culture believes it and lives by it does not make it scripturally sound. The ideology of Christ is absolute, but our human interpretation of it is marred by cultural and emotional perceptions, many of which damage the reputation of the unchanging reality.

This is exactly why Christ's mandate for us was to become less so that He could be seen as the Utmost. A God idea is concrete, but man's explanation of it is arbitrary. We come off less "God is the way" and more "See, I was right," and in so doing, communicate a prejudice against people rather than an intolerance for sin.

This is certainly not a shocker for God. He knew full well the direction mankind's tendencies would take us. In the midst of all this, He knew that there was still a way we could exemplify Christ to a world only capable of seeing the behavior of the humans who follow Him. But that method requires humility. It requires turning the other cheek. It requires living love, especially when no one is observing—because when we live love for an audience, it nurtures a heart that cares more for the philanthropic action itself than for the individual loved. It requires withholding our scathing verbal diatribes and instead living out a human example of the truth of the gospel. In short, we cannot truly exemplify godliness until we shut up.

Shortly after the Beatitudes (in fact during the same discourse), Jesus had some strong words for people of faith. He put us in our place before we even thought through what our place should be. In verse one of Matthew chapter 6, He makes our approach plain:

> Be careful not to do your "acts of righteousness" before men, to be seen by them. If you do, you will have no reward from your Father in heaven.

We haven't had a difficult time interpreting this passage to include our humanitarian efforts or our personal walk with Christ, but we've resisted applying it to our punditry. We are quick to wax eloquent about how our own supposed righteousness contrasts against those whom we deem as the villains of our day—the problem being that this act of decrying people is the part of our faith walk that is most under the microphone. Our very public attacking words aimed at people (people Jesus loves and died for) who disagree with us is under a megaphone. And the world is using our most irate voices to define us. They listen and they hear opinionated hatred, ignorance, antagonism, and of course hypocrisy—because we say our faith is one of love for all mankind, but we say it with a voice that is spitting bile.

Do I believe that Jesus would soften His stance on sin to today's audience? No way. Do I believe that Jesus would approach sinners with intimacy and tenderness? Absolutely. Jesus drew sinners to Himself. His love for them dissolved the hardness around their heart, and the heart would then begin the journey away from sin and toward Jesus. But we seem to have no interest in this approach. If we identify sin in someone else, we feel an urge to lead the conversation with that. We attack wrongness first as if that is the measure of Christlikeness when in actuality we aren't giving a lot of thought as to how Jesus would respond. Instead we are making certain that we are not culpable by association if anyone from the local church observes the conversation in question.

And yes, I am completely guilty of all of the above. My opinions are shaped by my faith, but also by my upbringing, my emotions, my prejudices—and those opinions quickly become my picture of God. They become unchecked rhetoric flowing from my mouth—atomic bombs damaging Christ's reputation—and I wave them willy-nilly as if it were my prerogative to be the official mouthpiece. It is far more difficult for me to take the time to discipline myself, immerse myself in Scripture, and to eradicate the inaccuracies of my thinking that have been tacked on to the truth *before* I speak.

We center so much of our Christian walk on the third parties: the people we disagree with. We make correcting those who disagree with us the backbone of our daily agenda. But Jesus was very particular about the third parties. Yes, He designed our lives to point the third parties to Him. Yes, He desires for us to go out and love those people to Him. But before we get to the third parties, He outlined a walk that gets it right with the first and second parties. *"Do not do your acts of righteousness before men."* He continues on a number of topics, all in Matthew 6:

> *When you give to the needy, do not announce it with trumpets, as the hypocrites do in the synagogues and on the streets, to be honored by men.*
>
> *When you give to the needy, do not let your left hand know what your right hand is doing, so that your giving may be in secret.*
>
> *When you pray, do not be like the hypocrites, for they love to pray standing in the synagogues and on the street corners to be seen by men.*
>
> *When you pray, go into your room, close the door and pray to your Father, who is unseen.*

Even when Jesus went so far as to teach us how to pray—giving us a note-for-note, beat-by-beat example—He did not make that prayer an eloquent attack on all that was wrong with the world while pleading with God to fix it. He barely made the prayer about the third parties at all—in fact only making it about them when we are giving them forgiveness. Instead He constructed the prayer as an exchange between the first and second parties: the first being God (the provider), and the second being us (the humbled and needy). The words of that prayer look nothing like our modern theological positioning. The Lord's Prayer does not sound like punditry. Those words, when prayed with sincerity, cannot help but put us in our place.

Our Father in heaven, hallowed be your name,
your kingdom come, your will be done
on earth as it is in heaven.
Give us today our daily bread.
Forgive us our debts, as we also have forgiven our debtors.
And lead us not into temptation,
but deliver us from the evil one.
For yours is the kingdom and the power and the glory
forever.

It is more than a prayer, really. It is an admission of know-nothingness on our part. An act of both contrition and complete humility. It is putting ourselves in our proper place: *God, You are God, and I am in need of sustenance, forgiveness, and deliverance that only You can provide.* It is a reminder that every human being is in that same predicament. Every single human has these same needs, and there is only one provider. He would love to utilize us to bring some of that provision to others in His name, but He cannot do so while our opinions take the God position in our lives. He can only do so when He is our one and only God.

It takes humility to come to Christ.

And it takes humility in us to breed humility in others.

When we come at the world with haughtiness, what exactly do we believe it is breeding?

It is breeding guile. It is breeding contempt and disillusionment.

In short it is priming a generation to hate Christians and therefore be spiritually unprepared to receive the truth of who Christ actually is and what He wants to do in their lives.

We may be angry at the sin, but we are taking it out on the sinner and, in so doing, hardening the shell around the behavior that is killing him.

THE ONLY CHANGE AGENT

We have a bad habit of presenting ourselves in a manner that seems to believe that righteousness is a change agent. It is *not*. Righteousness is the *goal*. *Jesus* is the only change agent. If a sinner collides with righteousness in an alleyway, he just backs up and takes another route. If a sinner collides with Jesus, Jesus embraces and does not let go.

Jesus was not a pundit, and it is evidenced in the way He approached the sinner. He did not prattle on condescendingly about the way a sinner should be improving. He saved those harsh words for the religious leaders. He spoke instead to the common man through stories. Stories that surprised the listener because they revealed an adept understanding of what the common man not only experienced in life, but processed in his or her mind and heart. Jesus' stories focused on actual need as opposed to perceived need. They commented on attitudes of the day while simultaneously upending them. Jesus positioned the prodigals as the sympathetic characters in the story, while forging an unchanging villain out of the holier-than-thou brothers who wanted the prodigal to get what they believed was coming to him. Jesus extended an olive branch to sinners, knowing that loving them closer would inevitably save them in entirety.

This particularly is missing in the way we are positioning Christianity to the public at large. We rarely display humility, kindness, love, or understanding. We are kicking and screaming at those who don't know Jesus, as if they were the Pharisees plotting to crucify Him. But Jesus set a different example. He expects us to love in a manner that is not positioned, to pray in a way that is not amplified over the loudspeaker, to speak in a way that is filled with humility and attempts at understanding. Our calling on this planet is to love people to Jesus.

Not scream them to Him.

Not complain them to Him.

Not know-it-all them to Him.

Not campaign or boycott them to Him.

To love them to Him.

As long as we insist on taking the adversarial approach, our name will say Christian while our words continually communicate the opposite.

It is only when that poison finally stops flowing out of our mouths that people will begin to see who Jesus truly is through the people who say they follow Him.

We will never lead the world to heaven until we finally shut up.

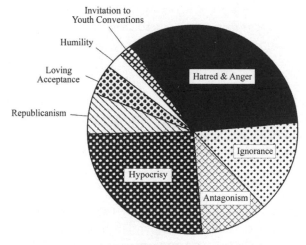

Invitation to
Youth Conventions

Humility

Loving
Acceptance

Republicanism

Hatred & Anger

Ignorance

Hypocrisy

Antagonism

**AN UNSCIENTIFIC BREAKDOWN
OF WHAT CHRISTIANS COMMUNICATE
THROUGH THEIR WORDS**

1. Consider the statement: *"My intelligence was accurate, but the method in which I had thrust that accuracy upon others made them resent both the truth and me."* Have you ever played either role in this equation?

2. Do you relate to the following statement: *"The modern church has been putting forth Christian thoughts with decidedly Christianish methods that turn the unchurched world off to any life-giving realities we might be purporting"*? Why or why not?

3. The ideology of Christ is absolute, but our human interpretation of it is marred by cultural and emotional perceptions, many of which damage the reputation of the unchanging reality. In what ways have you observed this in your own life and church community?

4. Why do you think it is so important to Christ that we do not do our acts of righteousness before men, especially if it could be a good witness?

5. The world listens to the church and *"they hear opinionated hatred, ignorance, antagonism, and of course hypocrisy—because we say our faith is one of love for all mankind, but we say it with a voice that is spitting bile."* What is our responsibility in this equation?

6. Consider and discuss the thought: *"It is far more difficult for me to take the time to discipline myself, immerse myself in Scripture, and eradicate the*

inaccuracies of my thinking that have been tacked on to the truth before I speak."

7. The Lord's Prayer puts us in our proper place: *"God, You are God, and I am in need of sustenance, forgiveness, and deliverance that only You can provide."* It is a reminder that every human being is in that same predicament. What does this say about the way we should live out our Christianity?

God said no   5

Baseball hates me.

And by "baseball," I don't mean the ideology. I refer to the actual round white orb. It hates me. I don't know what I did to offend it. It probably just smells the fear. I don't believe the fear is my fault, mind you. It comes from me being an object magnet.

Since an extremely early age, if something heavy was flying through the air, it would land on me. If something massive and stationary was near where I was moving, I would collide with it. This is how I crashed my bike into the lone, thin dogwood tree in our otherwise empty field of a front yard. Six times. In a single day. This is why I regularly step on the dog. This is why my car has been rear-ended by sleeping drivers twice. In a single year. This is why the grocery carts I push clip my poor wife on the sandaled heel. This is how I got 95 percent of a toothpick stuck straight down in the soft flesh of my foot between my big and second toe. And this is why, though I had a terribly difficult time catching footballs with my hands, I had no difficulty whatsoever in getting them lodged in my eye.

My body is a thing-sucker. I am my own planet with its own gravitational pull, and the satellites and asteroids are simply not staying put where they should.

This scientific anomaly intact, it is no surprise that I was never quite able to excel at athletics. This was a challenge growing up in Atlanta. In Georgia, boys have two potential career paths: playing baseball or destroying property. I loved baseball. I truly did, and I wanted to be good at it—no, great. But alas, I was not even passable. I observed my family as they watched each and every televised game, cheering and standing to their feet for champions they did not really know. I wanted to be one of those champions. To run the bases. To slide. To have my team sprint out to meet me at home plate and hoist me on their shoulders. But I did not have the first requirement for making this path possible. I did not have any athletic skill.

I loved the idea of most sports but hated playing. This was because sports hated me first. I was never as much a participant in the activities as I was a moving target. Others dogged me to suck it up and play anyway, but this was like saying that an elk has a bad attitude for not fondly anticipating hunting season.

To this end I thought I at least stood a chance at baseball. The whole game was about attracting the object, either to your glove or to the tip of your bat. If I could run into a fifth as many baseballs on purpose as I daily did on accident, I could single-handedly win the Little League World Series.

The reason I determined to give baseball in particular a try was because my father was such an aficionado of the pastime. In the days well before ESPN and its 212 derivatives, Atlanta had a local station owned by some wannabe named Ted Turner. The station (which went by the moniker WTBS) didn't have a lot going for it. I loved the channel because it had a sketch comedy show featuring Bill Tush and a pre-*SNL* Jan Hooks. The remainder of my family loved the network because it broadcast every Atlanta Braves game all season long. I enjoyed this for the most part, but prayed desperately for rain every Tuesday night so that we could occasionally flip over to a smidgen of *The A-Team*. Unfortunately, when it did rain, Dad would keep the channel on TBS in case God suddenly intervened.

Things had been different when we lived in Columbus, Georgia. While living there, my uncle had owned the local AAA franchise: the Columbus Astros. We spent many a spring and summer evening within that bricked circle, eating soft-serve ice cream out of upside-down batter's helmets and losing teeth on the gummy tip of Astro Pops. To this day, when I step on a discarded peanut shell, I am instantly taken back to the balmy evenings inside Astro Stadium—and then I open my eyes to realize I am actually at some unsanitary family steak house.

It was obvious by this immersion into the world of the game that my father put great precedence in his heart toward baseball. He had coached my oldest brother's baseball team and then he had coached my next-oldest brother's team. It only made sense that I would at least make the effort of a good son. This is why I went against my better judgment and offered to sign up to play.

DAV:	You want to what?
ME:	*I want to sign up to play baseball.*
DAV:	Do you know how to play baseball?

ME: *I want to sign up to learn how to play baseball.*

DAV: Well, they sort of expect you to know already.

My brothers gave me a crash course, which consisted of three key rules: 1) open the glove aimed at the oncoming ball instead of wearing the open glove on my head like an Easter bonnet, 2) do not hike up my pants so high that you cannot read my team's name on the tucked-in jersey, and 3) do NOT under any circumstances THROW the bat.

I especially had a difficult time with rule 3. Every time my bat would actually connect with the ball (a method I liked to call "accidental"), I would be in such a sudden panic to run that I would hurl the bat with all my might. Its trajectory tended to land it in the dugout where it would bounce about ceiling to wall until it had decapitated everyone.

BROTHER: DON'T THROW THE STUPID BAT, STUPID-
           HEAD!!

This was the counsel both brothers gave each and every time I batted—as each and every time I batted, I chucked that sucker like an Aussie expecting it to return back.

BROTHER: Do you want to cripple your teammates? Do you?

ME: *I don't know who my teammates are.*

BROTHER: Well, imagine they are people who would like to
           keep their heads.

ME: *I don't want to cripple anybody's head.*

BROTHER: Then stop CHUCKING the STUPID bat,
           STUPID-FACE!
ME: *I CAN'T HELP IT! I PANIC!*
BROTHER: DON'T PANIC, STUPID-PANIC-HEAD!

But I knew that I would. I panicked during every sport. When I played football, my head would get claustrophobic in the headgear and I would whip my neck back and forth, yearning for release. Instead the helmet would twirl clockwise just enough to render me blind. This is when the tackle would come.

In basketball I worked two full summers on my shot, only to discover that when other actual people were playing beside me, I would not only miss the backboard altogether, but a mascot would have to fetch the ball past the bleachers.

In dodgeball my panic would cause me to completely freeze (the only sport to have this effect). My gravitational pull would then cause the ball to hit me so hard in the temple that pieces of my soul would go flying out my ear.

I had a reputation as not only being bad at sports, but as being a sports killer—as in causing a team to lose so badly that all funding for the program was diverted to the knitting club. When we would play on the playground and I was the only choice left standing, the team would choose my imaginary friend before picking me.

I was that bad.

Hence, I was not surprised when I spent most of the forthcoming baseball season on the bench. For a while I felt special because the coach invented a new position for me: an infield/outfield hybrid called second-left-shortfielder. It was only slightly out-of-bounds just past the fence on the other side of the snack bar. I caught every ball that came to me, which was none, and racked up a monstrous tab for Lick 'Em Sticks.

Batting was another story, however, as my coach was required to include every player in the rotation, which meant every ninth hitter had to be me. This resulted in two missteps each time at bat. First, I would strike out in three solid swings. Second, I would throw the bat at the opposing team's dugout. This was never on purpose, and also never fared well. It would fling out of my hand, flitting about in a spiral like a helicopter blade, and then it would *(THUNK)* take out a chunk of concrete on the back wall of the dugout, barely missing turning Blaine Carson into a vegetable. I bet *that* would have messed with his perfect batting average and feathered bangs. This incident would transition seamlessly into a vein-popping shouting match between the opposing team's coach and the referee, who would then scold my coach, who would softly mutter "I know." When the melee dissipated, my coach (God bless him) would walk over to me, ruffle the hair on the top of my scalp, and say, "It's okay, kid. Only three more games."

As much as my coach (and team, and opposing team, and referee, and snack bar lady, whom I chatted up furiously) couldn't wait for the end of the season, neither could I. Baseball, though something I knew was life-giving for my family, was not at all life-giving for me. It was quite an anxiety-ridden experience, actually. I remember counting down the moments in that final game. It appeared that the batter before me was going to strike out, therefore finishing out the season before I would have to be humiliated (and potentially disembody someone) again.

No dice. He walked. It was going to be up to me.

You know the moment in all the sports movies when the team is going to lose unless someone hits a home run and it's the underdog's turn at bat? You know how suddenly everyone rallies around the underdog, giving him the energy to do that crazy movie act of unexpected sportsmanship that he has never shown the slightest ability toward accomplishing?

This was not that moment.

You know the moment in all the disaster movies where the watchman of the ship is staring into the fog and suddenly the peak of the iceberg appears about seven inches away and the watchman knows at that moment that he and all two thousand people on that boat are about to die a terribly ferocious death?

Yes. This was more like that.

As I stepped up to bat, the snack bar lady went ahead and hung up the "closed for the year" sign where her *99-cent nachos* wind sock had been. Other families in the stands were packing up their fold-out seat cushions. The umpire actually changed shirts. Slightly defeated, I reared my bat back and closed my eyes, imagining what B. A. Baracus might do in this situation. This led my mind astray into imagining how B. A. Baracus might actually defuse a bomb with tweezers and a number-two pencil while Howling Mad Murdock dressed up like a nun to distract passers-by.

CRAAACK!

I opened my eyes. What just happened? I had swung. I had SWUNG? My bat had connected with the ball! My mind went all aflutter. What was the rule? Oh yeah: Don't throw the STUPID bat, STUPID-HEAD. I tossed the bat gingerly to my immediate right and began to run. Elation! Sweet, grand elation! After what could only be described as a catastrophe of a season, I was finishing up with a miracle that would make Lazarus jealous. I was just about to step on first base when the umpire called out …

UMPIRE: HEY! Where's the fire?
ME: *What?*
UMPIRE: Get back here. It's a foul ball.

Ooooooooh. That made more sense.

I trudged back to home plate, hearing the occasional snicker coming from the opposing team's dugout and wondering if they would still be capable of snickering when the bat thrown by future-me inverted their cumulative teeth.

I stood behind the plate and began to choke up on the bat again, wondering if I could replicate the moment of near-Zen I had experienced by imagining a television action subplot instead of focusing on the forthcoming baseball. It was at that moment that I heard his voice:

DAD: *That's the way to do it, slugger!*

It was my dad.

In the midst of all the snickering and bored voices behind me, my father—who knew me well—applauded the fact that I stuck with the season long enough to finally connect with the ball, misguided connection though it was.

It was the juice of energy I needed. So I swung again.

Another foul. And another.

And another.

I finally struck out. A relief to everyone involved.

I had seen the season through. I would never play league baseball again.

I am aware that for many fathers, this seems a sad tale, but those fathers would be neglecting to observe the detail that the baseball hates me.

This is not a pity party. I have had more than my share of success in my lifetime, but zero of that success has had anything to do with the baseball. Because the baseball and I were never meant to pal around. I was not created to excel at baseball. And yes, I understand that if I had applied myself more—studied to show myself approved—I would have certainly improved over time. Perhaps I would have—like Sean Astin in *Rudy*—been tenacious enough to eventually be allowed onto a professional baseball field to stand with the other actual players with talent, pretending to live out my dream. But I did not do that. Because while others yearned for the pitcher's mound, my fingers ached for the 1954 manual typewriter covered on my desk upstairs. Yes—there were many potential pursuits in life that were flashier, more attractive to girls, more acceptable to Georgia culture—but only one pursuit that I knew in my depths I had a God-given yearning toward: writing. The other pursuits were not inherently wrong ...

... but for me, God said no.

When I composed stories or worked in the arts, I felt His glory and His truth being told. I did not feel this when I played sports. I wanted to. I wanted to excel, because everyone else did and I wanted the same opportunities and successes as everyone else. I wanted the ladies to faint over me like they did over the athletic savants. It would have made puberty much easier. But I was not meant to become a lowest common denominator: barely talented enough to blend in. I was meant to focus on God's unique design for my singularly unique life. And I was not the first.

UNIQUE DESIGN FOR A UNIQUE LIFE

All the way back to when Moses was climbing up Sinai to get those two stone tablets that set everything in motion, the people were clamoring to *do something*. To take action and be impressive. It's in our nature. We need to be defined and we simply cannot sit still. But God commanded the Israelites to do the single most difficult thing in the world—to wait. And while they waited forty days and nights for Moses and Joshua to come back down that mountain with the Law, they got so antsy in their nondoing that they built a false god and started worshipping it.

Hold on a second. What?

They melted and smelted a freaking false god and started worshipping it just because they were sick of not knowing what to do next?

Seriously?

That's just plain crazy.

And we scoff. But we also do the exact same thing.

We know God has a purpose for our individual lives, but we are uncomfortable waiting for that purpose to become crystal clear. So we create our own purposes of our own design—and then we worship the acts that we do—we worship what we accomplish instead of worshipping Christ.

God understood this antsiness in the Israelites, and when Moses came down that mountain, He gave the wanderers one more chance. He called the people to choose once and for all: Were they going to do their own thing or were they going to wait on the Lord? Those who chose themselves were quickly and succinctly destroyed. But that wasn't the end of the story. For those who chose God, He had acknowledged their need to *do something*, and He composed a plan in order to give them something *worth doing*.

God gave the people a plan for the very first mass artistic project intended to honor God: the tabernacle. God gave Moses all the details: exact measurements, a list of materials, a description of the furniture, some cherubim-print swatches, all the way down to specific colors. The people were eager and anxious to help, so God gave them a mandate for the first step:

> *Tell the Israelites to bring me an offering. You are to receive the offering for me from each man whose heart prompts him to give.*
>
> Exodus 25:2

Here's the clever part. The Israelites only had one treasure trove to give from: the plunder they had been rewarded by the Egyptians when Moses freed them. So put yourselves in the Israelites' sandals for a moment. You have been enslaved by an enemy nation your entire life. The hand of God finally frees you and, as you leave the enemy country, God gives you favor. The Egyptians, your former captors, shower you with gold and precious jewels and metals. In your mind this is finally payment in full for all the atrocities your people suffered under the Egyptians. This is salary plus bonus for a lifetime of servitude. You have no idea how long you're going to be in the wilderness, but you expect it will be a hop and a skip to the Promised Land, where you will begin your new life wealthy. Then God begins to list off the items needed in order to build the tabernacle. As these details tick away, you hear every item you gleaned from the Egyptians on this list. You hesitate, wondering what will come next, and then God drops the bomb: He wants you to surrender what you have, but only if your heart tells you so.

Oh snap.

This is extremely painful because up until recently, you were marked by nothing. You were an impoverished slave. Finally you *own* something and you cannot help but be a little bit defined by it. But just when you get used to that idea, God is asking you to surrender what you own—what He in fact gave you—in order to be a part of something larger. This is an uncomfortable thought. You ask yourself: How large a part am I going to play? If I surrender what I *have*, what does that mean? What next? What am I then going to be defined by? What is the thing that I will *do*?

This dysfunctional juggling act of defining who we are by what we have and what we do has been an epidemic in the Christian church for far too long. There is a hunger inside each of us and it is a hunger of belonging. Of fitting specifically into the place God designed for each of us. But we feed this hunger with the junk food of busyness and having. We accept every opportunity, follow every potential calling, volunteer for every good work, and own every acceptable knickknack we can get our hands on. But the hunger remains—and now we are too exhausted and our life too cluttered to be able to discern when the actual nourishing and intended food to fill that hunger of belonging comes along.

Fortunately for history the Israelites went against previous habit and gave freely. The coffers filled to overflowing, and Moses had more than enough to accomplish God's task. But the question remained in everyone's minds: Who would get to do each job?

Just like in modern life, some vocations and roles are flashier and more desirable than others, and this was certainly the case in the building of the tabernacle. In other words, who would want to dig holes when you could be selected for the artistic detail? To this end the high-profile positions in wilderness tabernacle-making were the most desired, and there was no shortage of Israelites eager to fill those roles. The catch is: Most of them were not meant to fill those roles. As a matter of fact, out of all the Israelites wandering in the wilderness, God had paved this particular plan for only a handful.

The first were named Bezalel and Oholiab, and they are two of my favorite people in the Bible. Why? Because they identified and followed the very specific path for which they were created. You see, Bezalel had God-given talent. He was one of the earliest designers. We read in the book of Exodus how the Lord *"filled [Bezalel] with the Spirit of God, with skill, ability and knowledge in all kinds of crafts—to make artistic designs for work in gold, silver and bronze, to cut and set stones, to work in wood and to engage in all kinds of artistic craftsmanship" (Ex. 35: 31–33).*

But here's the real aha: It is certainly rational to assume that Bezalel developed this God-given gift the same way we all develop our God-given gifts—throughout his entire life, long before it ever made sense to him how it could or would be used for God's glory.

He simply realized what God made him to do, and he pursued it passionately while pursuing God even more so. To this end, when it came time to build the tabernacle, Bezalel was the prime candidate for the glory job. Talk about an underdog tale. In an age where this sort of manual labor was not exactly seen as an upper-class pursuit, Bezalel perfected his art, never thinking in the back of his mind, *I will become an expert bronze worker because one day, I will spearhead the most publicized faith-based bronze project of all time.* He pursued it simply because it was what the Creator made him to pursue. What is perhaps more important is what Bezalel was *not* good at. He was an expert at fine metals, stones, and crafts, yes. But other than that, he held no position. He was not a Levite. He did not have leadership status. He was not significant or popular in his tribe. He was simply solid and developed at his one thing. And then, all of a sudden, his one thing became important.

This is the opposite of how we position individuals in the modern church, because we do not begin with God's purpose for individuals in mind. We begin with projects. Or, scratch that, we begin with perceived success in other ministries or other Christians' lives, and follow that perception by attempting to emulate their projects. Once we feel we have come upon a potentially successful project, we front-load it with as many amiable volunteers as possible, regardless of whether or not they fit—simply because they want to fit. We do not help others find their one thing. Rather, we expect them in the name of Christ to be willing to do everything. It is a "Leave No Christian Behind" approach to communicating the gospel and it normally results in some form of interpersonal disaster. I don't know when this all began, but at some point we started feeling bad that not everyone had figured out how they fit into the kingdom of God. At this juncture we had two options as a community:

1. Take the time to help one another discover God's plan for their life, or
2. Let everyone do everything they want to do.

Guess which one we chose. We have become the church of the perpetual yes (unless of course, you come from outside the church— but that's a different story). No one wants to say no to someone who wants to help in the work of the Lord, so everyone gets an affirmative. We expect this will allow everyone to feel good and therefore commit to volunteer or assist even more. To this end it seems that a great amount will be accomplished effectively. But alas, this is often not the result—because when a human works in a manner that human was not designed to work, said human senses the reality of not fitting. When one does not fit, one feels useless, discouraged, incapable, overworked, underappreciated, and unfortunately just as empty as one felt prior to the inappropriate yes. Of course, it is far more difficult to place people in their proper roles in the first place. It requires a deeper knowing, a more severe community. In other words, it requires the church to understand each other before each other does anything.

God certainly didn't give blank-check yeses. When the tabernacle was about to get underway, everyone was clamoring for an important job. That's when God introduced the Israelites to Bezalel and Oholiab.

Then Moses said to the Israelites, "See, the LORD has
chosen Bezalel son of Uri, the son of Hur, of the tribe
of Judah, and he has filled him with the Spirit of God,
with skill, ability and knowledge in all kinds of crafts—
to make artistic designs for work in gold, silver and
bronze, to cut and set stones, to work in wood and to
engage in all kinds of artistic craftsmanship. And he has
given both him and Oholiab son of Ahisamach, of the
tribe of Dan, the ability to teach others. He has filled
them with skill to do all kinds of work as craftsmen,
designers, embroiderers in blue, purple and scarlet yarn
and fine linen, and weavers—all of them master crafts-
men and designers. So Bezalel, Oholiab and every skilled
person to whom the LORD has given skill and ability to
know how to carry out all the work of constructing the
sanctuary are to do the work just as the LORD has com-
manded." Then Moses summoned Bezalel and Oholiab
and every skilled person to whom the LORD had given
ability and who was willing to come and do the work.

Exodus 35:30—36:2

God had Moses summon the people who had two crucial quali-
fications: willingness and skilled ability. Follow me here. This is not
an elitist view. This is a "put people in the correct place" view. True,
it is difficult in many cases to determine what role someone is created
for in God's plan, but that difficulty does not make it a moot point.
That difficulty, rather, makes it an issue deserving of great attention
and affection. But in the modern church world, we have all but

eradicated an approach that gets to know the individuals enough to direct them in their God-ordained purpose. Instead we tend to throw them at everything and see what sticks—or worse yet, we empower them to do the thing for which they have the most "desire."

This desire approach—gee, it sure would work if we based our desires on first seeking God through Scripture and prayer, but we don't do that. We tend to base our desire on our emotions. We call it our passion. If something moves us, we want to be a part of it—and we want to be *noticed* as a part of it—and we want to be an *important* part of it—and we want to be an important part of it *immediately* without process, training, or rehearsal. To this end we continue to stick people in places where they either fail or flail. This is why the modern church is so filled with subpar copies of successful things instead of uniquely unproven and different things.

The truth is, God says no.

He said no to the thousands who wanted the creative role in building the tabernacle, and He said yes to a small handful—a handful who had been developing those specific skills their entire lives without knowing *why* they needed to be developing them. Bezalel and Oholiab became excellent in the arts because it was *inside* them—and it was inside them because that was the way God built them.

ME BLOCKING ME

So now the obvious follow-up question:

Why do so many people today find it so difficult to uncover what God built them to do?

This is one of the most significant questions in the modern church. It leads directly to the "why am I so unhappy" question, the "where do I really fit in" question, and the "why won't God answer me" question. The answer isn't necessarily pleasant.

In modern Christianity we aren't seeing what God made us each to be because we are each blinded by our self.

God has created us each unique—and God is consistently speaking in order to clarify that uniqueness. God has put His clues all over each of us: in the things that energize us and make us tick. But somehow most of us still can't see what we label "the calling." Why? Because we each have too much *me* standing in the way.

Too many emotions.

Too many instant and available pleasures.

Too much entertainment and stimulation.

Too many amusements that never quite tackle the boredom.

Too many options we have attempted to try.

We do not tend to get down to the quiet self. The base level of intimacy between God and our silent soul—a soul that has been stripped of all the fraudulent influences that will attempt to deceive us into thinking we deserve something we don't or should be something we are not. Instead we bask in the noise and the stimulation of modern life so much that if someone were to ask us what makes us tick, it would be equally true to answer "everything" or "nothing." We expect God to give us answers while on the basest level, God keeps saying no to the things to which we keep saying yes. Amid this much noise-induced apathy, how can we identify the sort of truth that Bezalel knew simply because it was the only obvious answer for him?

Simple. We do not identify it in ourselves.

We cannot.

There is too much noise.

Instead we identify it in one another.

When one stares at his or her own life, there is too much confusion to make sense of it. It is too personal, too emotional. However, if another person, perhaps a friend, stands at a close distance—inserted into the life of the other enough to truly know them without the muddy self-deception—suddenly that person is able to see the other's true worth. I have certainly seen this reality in my own life. In the seasons where I was uncertain which path to take, which "calling" to pursue, God placed trustworthy individuals into my life to get to know me, and in knowing, to earn a place to both identify and speak into my next step. This assumes, of course, that we are each putting ourselves in a position where others can identify God at work in our lives: Namely, we are actively and vulnerably loving. If we each want to have God's plan for us identified, then we first have to set down all of the projects and the programs and get back to the base commandment of loving the people in our everyday lives. It is amazing how quickly our perspective of forward motion improves when we stop obsessing on the stunted and stale self and instead focus our energies on noticing the hurting others in our immediate surroundings and doing something simple to love them. It is through these generous actions that those in our circle are able to identify how God has skilled us. It becomes obvious through the fruits of effective loving. This requires an individual-first approach to ministry instead of a mass-response approach.

But it is *vital* because—in the meantime—the all-hands-on-deck approach isn't doing Christianity any favors.

Some of the most significant damage done to the credibility of Jesus' message has been the slipshod approach of conveying it by many of His followers. Though there are a significant amount of Christ-followers who have shown excellence in their art and business, the percentages of crappy art and bad business justified with the name of Jesus are staggeringly high. We have made cheeseball films and abhorrent television, believing that an altar call at the end means it won't return void. We have produced derivative music for a dime, putting a capital Y on the "you" in the love song and calling it worship. We have made questionable (and oft illegal) financial decisions at the helm of ministries, defending the action by the evangelistic ends justifying the means. We have mistreated people standing in the way of our goal, berated people who disagreed with our goal, and stepped on good people to climb to our goal—all in the name of Christ. Why? All because people keep trying to fit where God did not create them to fit.

And Jesus is the one getting the black eye over it.

This all may seem a bit harsh, but the Bible is actually very clear on the subject. In the first book of Corinthians, chapter 3, beginning in verse 10, Paul paints a brilliant analogy about the strength of our faith. He describes it as a building with a proper foundation. But he pushes even further to state, *"each one should be careful how he builds."* Not just *what* he builds, but *how*—because the process and the skill we apply (even in our faith) has eternal ramifications. He continues with *"no one can lay any foundation other than the one already laid, which is Jesus Christ. If any man builds on this foundation using gold, silver, costly stones, wood, hay or straw, his work will be shown for what it is, because the Day will bring it to light. It will be revealed with fire, and the fire will test the quality of each man's work."* Big. Fat. Ouch.

So it has to begin with Jesus. It always has to begin with Jesus. His calling. His plan. His purpose. We must take the time and the necessary means to uncover how we each fit into this puzzle of a world. For Bezalel it was his artistry. What then is it for me? Once we uncover this purpose, we cannot stop there, for Paul has made it clear that *how* we build on Christ's foundation is every bit as important. Our excellence. Our care for the other people in the path.

This is where Jesus was an utmost example for us. When God sent His Son to earth to live, you would have thought that He could have given Jesus the most significant, esteemed, and high-profile occupation on the planet. This, of course, He did not do. Instead He gave Him a humble calling that He did exceedingly well. The Creator allowed His Son to follow in the family business. To create. This is why Jesus built stuff.

Jesus was a carpenter. Not simply so He would be relatable. It was how He fed himself and had a place to lay His head. He learned the trade from His earthly father and was accomplished at it. So accomplished, in fact, that it gave Him a place to speak to the common man. Suddenly they saw someone speaking truth who did not seem to come from hierarchy. Here was a man who was not only void of elitism, but He had rough, calloused hands just like theirs. He didn't just speak of the ordinary person God loved, He also seemed like one Himself. Here was a man who understood both love and hard work. A man who understood excellence and stopping to embrace another along the occupational journey. Jesus was not defined by what He did for a dime. What He did for a dime was defined by who Jesus was. In the meantime His ethic and His excellence were community currency that purchased respect and admiration. It gave Him a voice to some who would not have otherwise listened. It is reminiscent of words Paul would not write down until much later:

> *Make it your ambition to lead a quiet life, to mind your own business and to work with your hands, just as we told you, so that your daily life may win the respect of outsiders and so that you will not be dependent on anybody.*
>
> 1 Thessalonians 4:11–12

Of all the human beings in the history of the planet who had a caveat to be exempt from this verse, it would have been Jesus. He had every right, and some would say, every need for His vocational role to be the most public and admired of anyone's. But instead He was a carpenter. That's because Jesus understood the proper role for what one *does*. Jesus did not come to earth as a politician, a spokesperson, a pastor, or a reality television star. He arrived as a fellow in your neighborhood. The fellow you come to listen to because He earns your respect by His understanding of the role He plays on this earth and by the excellence in which He embraces that role. Jesus knew that He was destined to save the world. To this end He could have looked at the menial, seemingly unimportant task of building houses as something He could blow off in order to get cracking on that evangelism before the age of thirty. Instead He adhered to wisdom that would not be written until well after His death:

Whatever you do, work at it with all your heart, as
working for the Lord, not for men.

Colossians 3:23

Jesus got the whole work idea. We don't do it with all our heart as working for the Lord merely because the Lord is watching. We also do it with all our heart working for the Lord because the *world* is watching. And when the world sees that the way we work is different from the way they work, they may just get the idea that we are doing it for a greater purpose than defining ourselves.

I did eventually get to run the bases in a real game. It was a trivial moment, actually. Important to no one but myself. I was in college, watching our championship team play as the game was rained out by a monsoon. Just as the crowd began to dissipate, the commentator blared over the loudspeaker,

ANNOUNCER: Is there a Mark Steele in the stadium? The players would like for Mark Steele to come down to the dugout of the home team.

Flabbergasted (as I was in awe of the baseball team), I wandered down to discover that the game had been called and the team was about to run the muddy bases in the downpour—a yearly ritual.

They wanted to know if I would like to take part.

I did my best to remain cool and collected, and nodded affirmatively. Inside, I was having panic flashbacks to fouling out. I certainly hoped no skill would be involved.

Once on the diamond my fears were whisked away as I saw the guys playing with no actual bats or balls. I walked to the plate as the commentator blared over the loudspeaker,

ANNOUNCER: Now batting for the Titans, pinch hitter Mark
Steele!

The remnant of the crowd who remained—mostly a few guys from my wing and the completely mortified girl I was dating at the time—cheered wildly as I mock swung and then ran the bases in a trench of mud, diving through the water and filth like a pig at Woodstock. As I rounded third and ran for home, the entire team sprinted out to home plate in mock celebration as if I had just secured the pennant. They hoisted me on their shoulders as the somewhat limited crowd chanted, *"Steele Steele Steele."*

Drying off inside the locker room, I pulled my own friend on the team aside to ask if he had been the instigator of the incident.

BRETT: No way, bro. It was the whole team. The guys saw
you in the stands and they wanted you down here.

This made zero sense to me. I had gone through life without the slightest athletic ability. I did not know these gentlemen, and certainly did not frequent the same social circle. What reason could they possibly have had to bring me, the team-killer, onto their turf— their vocation—their field?

BRETT: You inspire them, man.

ME: *How could I possibly inspire them? I don't even know*
           them.

BRETT: It was something you wrote, Steele. Something
           you wrote.

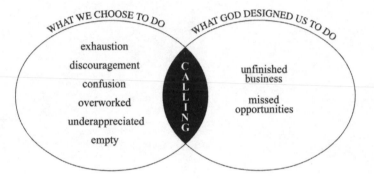

1. Can you identify the things in your life that seem
like good things on the surface, but are actually
golden calves standing between you and God's real
calling for your life?

2. Can you identify with the sentiment of being
marked as someone who has nothing? What do you
then do when God gives you something, but requires
it surrendered back to Him? Do you find yourself
asking the questions: *"If I surrender what I have,
what does that mean? What next? What am I then
going to be defined by? What is the thing that I will
do?"*

3. Do you struggle with finding self-worth in what
you accomplish instead of in the knowledge that you
belong to God? Why do you think this is true?

4. Do you agree with the following statements: *"We
feed the hunger of belonging with the junk food of
busyness and having. We accept every opportunity,
follow every potential calling, volunteer for every
good work, and own every acceptable knickknack we
can get our hands on. But the hunger remains—and
now we are too exhausted and our lives too cluttered
to be able to discern when the actual nourishing
and intended food to fill that hunger of belonging
comes along"*? Why or why not?

5. Do you ever struggle with jealousy over God's
calling on other Christians?

6. Consider Bezalel: an individual who was faithful to pursue his God-ordained "one thing" his

entire life, diligently and with excellence, having no idea it would one day become important. Does this inspire you to pursue your one thing rather than everything?

7. Have you ever taken a role in church where you did not truly fit? What was the result of this effort?

8. What are the negative repercussions of being a "church of the perpetual yes"?

9. Discuss the desire approach: *"We tend to base our desire on our emotions. We call it our passion. If something moves us, we want to be a part of it— and we want to be noticed as a part of it—and we want to be an important part of it—and we want to be an important part of it immediately without process, training, or rehearsal."* Has this ever described you?

losers for Jesus   6

My wife, Kaysie, and I like to go the same places, but we don't like to get there the same way. When driving together in the same vehicle, we will argue ad nauseam which route is the quickest path to our destination. We comprehend that this is a normal male-female discourse, but matters are not helped by the fact that we live in Tulsa: a town full of square grids. There is not a locale within a twenty-mile radius that does not have at least three practically equidistant approaches. This, of course, means that Kaysie and I will argue each other to the floorboards over whose course is most accurate.

KAYSIE: Mark, you should take 169 to I-44.

ME: *I'm taking 169 the other way, down to Riverside.*

KAYSIE: Why would you do that? You do realize we're heading downtown.

ME: *Of course I realize we're heading downtown. I drive downtown every day. At this time of evening, the traffic on I-44 will be crushing.*

KAYSIE:	Except that there is construction on Riverside.
ME:	*Which is why most cars are avoiding Riverside and taking I-44.*
KAYSIE:	Because those cars are using their brains.

It's even worse on evenings when we take separate cars, meeting after work. Inevitably on the ride back home, Charlie will want to ride with Daddy and Charlie will want to *race*. This is because Charlie has heard all previous traffic arguments between Mommy and Daddy, and Charlie wants to know that Daddy knows what he is talking about, and Charlie wants all men to win. This is when the mature decision comes in to play. I have three choices:

1. Drive my current route normally and discover who was actually correct.
2. Drive my current route while speeding to prove Kaysie wrong.
3. Second-guess my current route and venture a third option.

I select option 2. I am a man. And this means that I need to be proven right by all means necessary, even if those means include bending the law a smidge. Unfortunately, even after rushing home through every technically yellow light, *if* I happen to win, it is by mere nanoseconds. And then of course, what do I win? I win making her upset that I sped home just to prove her wrong. I win nothing.

My addiction to being correct began at an early age. I didn't like most board games, because there always tended to be some moronic rule that kept me from coming in first place. This is why I spent a great deal of my childhood bedroom time building my own board games. Each focused on a skill that I alone excelled at and contained a wealth of regulations that only I could remember and were flexible to change during game play at the bidding of the gamemaster (me).

Unfortunately no one ever wanted to play these games, calling them "unfair," "lopsided," and "difficult to play due to the dice being made out of notebook paper and glue stick." It dawned on me that a board game that skewed to myself as winner didn't do me any good if there were no potential losers willing to play, so I made a secondary plan.

It was a Saturday evening, and I had finally convinced my parents and brothers to play Family Feud. It was the home version, which meant that the box came with a tiny plastic replica of the big tally board that normally hovered over the head of Richard Dawson. The home version came with a stack of a hundred cards that could only be read properly if inserted into the master board. This kept the host from seeing the answers and allowed me to be both emcee and contestant. Simultaneous leader and follower. My favorite hierarchy. I was stoked and my family was amicable enough to join in.

We were playing the updated 1977 edition, which meant there were a lot of Farrah Fawcett and Jimmy Carter questions. My mother quickly ripped the card out of the game that read "what is the strangest place you've ever made whoopee," leading my brothers and me to believe that whoopee was a dessert treat we were not allowed to taste. After my parents dominated the question about "top ten ways to mispronounce Ayatollah," my team was losing the game. I knew it was finally time for my secret weapon.

I unveiled the next question: "What is your favorite Bugs Bunny character?" My brother Dav (who was on my team) quickly said "Bugs Bunny." It was the number one answer.

My mother looked intently at the word written on the number one slot of the master board.

MOM:	Mark?
ME:	*Yep?*
MOM:	Isn't that your handwriting?
ME:	*Hmm?*
MOM:	On the board. The answer board. Where it says "Bugs Bunny." Isn't that your handwriting?
ME:	*Yep.*
MOM:	You wrote this question yourself?
ME:	*Uh-huh.*
MOM:	And all the answers.
ME:	*Mm-hm.*
MOM:	So, when it says, "People were surveyed and the top seven answers are on the board," the people it's talking about—that's just you.
ME:	*And Dav.*
MOM:	But Dav's also on your team.
ME:	*Yes.*
MOM:	Isn't that against the rules?
ME:	*Well—I'm the host.*
MOM:	But you're also a contestant.
ME:	*I'm also the host.*

And the game continued. Needless to say, the Mark-Dav team absolutely dominated that particular question. We not only selected every correct answer, we selected every correct answer in the correct order of popularity. This did not go over well with the opposing team. Yes, we technically won, but in the eyes of the competition, we had cheated. Dav and I did not consider this cheating. After all, the question was not "what are the best Bugs Bunny characters." The question was "what are the group's favorite Bugs Bunny characters." Dav and I were the group, so Dav and I knew the answers. We had the inside scoop. Extremely inside. We should not have been penalized just because the other team did not know what was inside us as well as we did. To this end Dav and I were confident that we had won—but most importantly we were thrilled that we had been proven correct.

And that is the rush, isn't it? That we each be proven accurate or correct. We place the lion's share of our actions and reactions on reinforcing what we believe and dismantling the ways others see things differently. Belief is our power and conviction is our megaphone. We have less of a tendency to reveal God's truth as much as we have a burning-hot desire to prove our own beliefs accurate.

Do not misunderstand me. There is only one absolute truth and that truth is Jesus Christ. He is the only way to God, and He carries justice and grace with Him in equal measure. But this isn't the issue being debated. Somewhere along the way, we have each decided that not only is Jesus absolute truth, but that our limited understanding of His vastness is also. We never stop to realize that, yes, a great deal of what we each understand Christ to be comes from Scripture—but that understanding is also either reinforced or tainted with outside influences:

- our own life experiences
- the convincing words of other people
- our prejudices and life patterns
- our emotions

In other words, everything about Jesus is absolute, but that doesn't mean that everything *you think about Him* is absolute. You and I are human, and the chance that either of us, in our limited understanding of an infinite God, has it completely dead-on accurate—is 0 percent.

The beauty is this: You and I don't need to fully comprehend every detail of His grandeur in order to trust Christ and live for Him. On the contrary, it is a greater sign of faith that we as humans choose to surrender our lives to an omnipotent Savior who is beyond our measure of understanding. The danger lies when one deceives himself into believing he has it exactly right. At this point one cannot help but stop worshipping the real God, and instead worship the details of the God in his own imagination. One will find himself defending that mental picture by all means necessary in order to prove himself correct, even if he has to bend God's law a smidge in order to do so.

This is where the unreached world's picture of Christians comes from. When they say we are opinionated and closed-minded, what they actually are saying is that there is no life to our arguments, only a selfish protection to one's opinion. We say we are all about a God that loves—about a Savior who died for all—but we treat anyone with an opposing discourse as enemy. We prickle in order to prove wrong instead of attempting to woo others to the truth. We have become antagonistic and unreachable, proselytizing our own accurateness instead of Christ's goodness.

THE PAINFUL GIVE

Our current cultural state most resembles the moment in Matthew chapter 19 when a young man who had everything came to Jesus and asked what it would take to have eternal life. Christ told the man to obey the commandments. When the man inquired as to which ones, Jesus answered …

> *"Do not murder, do not commit adultery, do not steal, do not give false testimony, honor your father and mother," and "love your neighbor as yourself."*

The man, feeling pretty good about himself at that point, told Jesus that he had kept all of those commandments. What was there left that he had not done? That's when Jesus dropped the bomb:

> *If you want to be perfect, go, sell your possessions and give to the poor, and you will have treasure in heaven. Then come, follow me.*

And the young man went away sad, because he had great wealth. Yeah. He got served. That's when Jesus told His disciples that it would be easier for a camel to go through the eye of a needle than for a rich man to enter the kingdom of God.

We've all heard this story before and it has been utilized often to paint a picture for both philanthropic giving and living an open-handed life, both of which are important pursuits. But there is a more subtle truth here as well.

Yes, Jesus harped specifically on earthly wealth with this young man, but one of the reasons this was certainly the approach was because earthly wealth was what this young man actually *had.* Earthly wealth was his point of strength and value and confidence. When the beggars came to Jesus, He didn't drop the same gauntlet. He didn't ask them to sell their few meager belongings and follow Him. Jesus always asked for the painful give. From a blind man, Christ required faith. From a prostitute, Christ valued innocent and untainted affection like tears on His feet. From Pharisees, He required an abandonment of their hypocrisy, and from the disciples (the ones who thought they knew the most about Jesus and were closest to Him)—from them, Jesus required a move to the back of the line. In Mark chapter 9, as the disciples rattled on, arguing endlessly about which of them was the greatest in Christ's eyes, Jesus' response to them was this:

> *If anyone wants to be first, he must be the very last,*
> *and the servant of all.*

We certainly don't perceive that we go about in modern culture with an attitude of "which of us is the greatest," but the reality is that we do. We are not more immune to that temptation than those who walked daily with Jesus Himself. The truth is, we serve Jesus with very little openness to how He might mess with our perception of Him. Instead we lock in our opinion and daily chase that opinion, with very little love for those who oppose, and very little malleability to allow Jesus to upend our thinking. We reach a point in our Christian walk where it would be too embarrassing to discover we were wrong about some detail. So we don't allow teachableness to thrive. We choke it out and call it conviction. We close our mind with cement so that we cannot hear an opposing view without the bile hitting the top of our throat and our blood pressure rising a half-dozen points. The bitter outcome is that we stop hearing Jesus and we start hating those who don't follow Him.

Christ demanded the wealth of the rich young ruler because it was his protection. It was what he trusted more than God. Yes, there is a sin issue prevalent in craving wealth, and we will get to that in the next chapter, but methinks Christ would demand something different from you and me. Something we hold much more valuable than the things we own. Christ would demand instead the thing that we hide behind. He would demand the wall wedged between Him and us.

Christ would demand that we surrender our precious opinion.

RIGHTNESS OVER RIGHTEOUSNESS

We believe it is our right to be right. Yes, we are supposed to have convictions and we are supposed to stand strongly upon the truth we know. Solid convictions lead us to live a holy life. But that is not what seems to be happening in American Christianity. In modern faith our certainty has replaced love. A healthy faith walk is a collision of both.

Enough certainty and conviction to walk out life pursuing Christ and holiness—but enough love to draw others (even those who do not agree with our conviction) to Christ. Conviction without love is just an angry opinion. Conviction with love proves that what is true is also alive. That it is not only a code, but a transformative power. Conviction alone needs desperately to be proven accurate at all costs. In short, it only survives when it wins. And unfortunately for our opinion, Christ has called us to be losers.

Humility.

It's certainly not one of the top three pulpit topics of the decade, but it was one of the most integral themes to all of Jesus' teaching. As a matter of fact, these two alone would have to be among the most unpopular of Christ's teachings among the modern church:

> *You have heard that it was said, "Eye for eye, and tooth for tooth." But I tell you, Do not resist an evil person. If someone strikes you on the right cheek, turn to him the other also. And if someone wants to sue you and take your tunic, let him have your cloak as well. If someone forces you to go one mile, go with him two miles. Give to the one who asks you, and do not turn away from the one who wants to borrow from you. You have heard that it was said, "Love your neighbor and hate your enemy." But I tell you: Love your enemies and pray for those who persecute you, that you may be sons of your Father in heaven. He causes his sun to rise on the evil and the good, and sends rain on the righteous and the unrighteous.*

> Matthew 5:38–45

Do not judge, or you too will be judged. For in the
same way you judge others, you will be judged, and
with the measure you use, it will be measured to
you. Why do you look at the speck of sawdust in your
brother's eye and pay no attention to the plank in your
own eye? How can you say to your brother, "Let me
take the speck out of your eye," when all the time there
is a plank in your own eye? You hypocrite, first take the
plank out of your own eye, and then you will see clearly
to remove the speck from your brother's eye.

Matthew 7:1–5

Say that again? If someone hits me once, let him hit me again? If someone wants to sue me for what I own, give him even more? Do not judge? Love my enemy? This can't be serious. I mean, we are all acutely aware of these teachings. We have heard these sermons a couple dozen times since childhood and they were always accompanied by some cute flannelgraph that insinuated the teaching was limited to giving Sunday school friend Bobby a hug to resolve a conflict. But these days? Well, I can't say that I've allowed this teaching to seep too deeply into my daily actions. My own responses tend to correspond with the rest of the modern church. If someone hits me, I want to get even. If someone wants to sue me, I want to prove him wrong. I judge all the time. I may not say it out loud, but every time someone disagrees with my perception of God, I love them a little bit less. And love my enemies? What benefit is there in that? If someone hurts me, I want them to hurt—and if someone disagrees with my perception of God, I want God to strike them with some holy lightning right where they stand.

But look at that last Scripture again: *Do not judge, because the measure of judgment you use will be measured back to you.*

Whoa.

Do you mean to tell me that every time I size up someone based on my perception of reality—every time I discount someone's life and worth because they disagree with my take on matters—every time I notch them downward, I am spiraling myself the same?

This exposes the give that Christ is demanding of the modern church. We ask what it means to have eternal life and we desperately want to know how to follow Him. To this He has an answer: We must give up that with which we are protecting ourselves. We must humble ourselves and surrender our precious opinion. This does not mean that we stop standing up for the truth. It means simply that we stand up in truth while we simultaneously stand up in love. That we bridge the gap between those we would inaccurately call our enemies. That instead we would allow the reality of the truth to drive us to sacrifice, to be willing to *not* be proven right.

I don't know when this competitive urge for Christians to get the win started, but it's made an awful mess of things. It may have been when we stopped pursuing Jesus and instead began picking sides. After all, the Beatitudes don't tend to look a lot like modern Christianity. We choose a political team. We select a denominational preference. We hitch our cart to a branch of philosophy. Anyone that disagrees is quickly and succinctly judged, and simultaneously disregarded as worthless.

Big problem with that approach.

We are supposed to be loving those who don't agree with us to Jesus—and you can't love those whom you deem worthless.

Perhaps it is time to redefine worth.

Up until now (though we would never think it true), we have defined others around us on a scale ranging the gamut of wrongness to rightness. I don't know how we have decided what the harbinger of this scale is. It's supposed to be Christ and Christ alone, which means that He is the only one with enough inside scoop to make the call—but that doesn't seem to stop any of us from making the assessment of others anyway.

In this vein of thinking, we each treat ourselves as if we were a "ten:" someone who has the pursuit of Christ completely figured out and is doing his or her best to follow accordingly. This, of course, is irrational. None of us have enough information to know whether or not we are a ten. And if we cannot know for certain that we are a ten, how can we then fairly "rank" anyone else?

This is how planet Earth earned its shameful reputation of undervaluing people by ethnicity, religion, gender, and whatnot. At some point man's impression was labeled the voice of God. But man's impression always contained the blind flaw of humanness. Now here we are in the twenty-first century doing the exact same thing: making personal assessments of one another based on our limited understanding of a supernatural reality that we could not possibly completely fathom. We are ranking people "ones" and "threes," or (if they're lucky) "nines" based on the barometer of our own faith as the desired "ten." Talk about grading on a false curve.

Time for a new scale.

If we do not have the insight to observe real truth, we should mark what we can observe: a loved and therefore transformed life.

This is a ranking worth assessing, because it is a ranking that prompts us to action—action that is inherently good.

A life bridged from one spectrum (an alienation toward God and people who follow Him) to the other (a life fully committed to following Christ), requires steps. We tend to dismiss these steps by feeling animosity toward anyone who opposes us. But the truth is, the more someone opposes the path following Christ, the more he needs to be loved by those who truly do follow Christ.

Everyone is somewhere along that scale. Some are low on the scale: alienated and angry at God because of the mistakes of other human beings. Some have head knowledge but don't believe it is real. Others know but do not care. Some want the truth to be real, but don't know how to take a first step. For all those lives that represent any of these stages along the path to Christ, Jesus expects us to have a specific response. That response is one of love.

Why does Jesus demand that we turn the other cheek, that we not retaliate or judge? Because on a human level, it is unexpected. We say that we serve the real God, the unchanging truth, the epitome of love. But then, when we encounter antagonism, we respond like any other normal human being without God. Jesus knows what the world knows: It is easy to say you love Jesus when you feel nothing but affection back. The real test of what is actually truth is how we respond when the only thing we get back is the opposite of love. Are we still willing to share the love of Christ? Are we willing to be humbled—or even perceived as wrong?

The truth is, the path to Christ is not a game about winners and losers. It is about finishers who refuse to abandon the difficult path mid-race when it requires them to help carry others to the finish line.

Scratch that: It might just be about the losers as well. The ones who were willing to crush their own pride and embrace humility. Those who did not need the win or to be proven right, but rather had a desperate desire to see what Jesus sees: a hurting world filled with disillusioned people whom Jesus continues to love. Jesus loves them, though they batter the people who follow Him, though they throw tantrums and blame, though they feel deep down as if they hate everything about those who call themselves Christians.

Jesus loves those people.

Jesus wants us to reach those people.

But those people can only be reached by those of us who are first willing to lose.

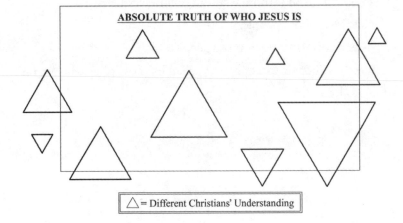

ABSOLUTE TRUTH OF WHO JESUS IS

△ = Different Christians' Understanding

1. Have you ever found it true that Christians have less of a tendency to reveal God's truth as much as we have a burning-hot desire to prove our own beliefs accurate? What's the difference?

2. *"Everything about Jesus is absolute, but that doesn't mean that everything you think about Him is absolute. You and I are human, and the chance that either of us, in our limited understanding of an infinite God, has it completely dead-on accurate—is 0 percent."* Agree or disagree?

3. Have you ever found yourself vehemently defending your emotional understanding of God outside of Scripture?

4. Do you find yourself pursuing Jesus, regardless of how He may upend your daily thinking? Do you lock in your personal opinion of Jesus and daily chase that opinion, with very little love for those who oppose, and very little malleability to allow Jesus to upend those beliefs?

5. How teachable are you in your current walk of faith? From your spiritual authorities? From those on your own level? From those with whom you disagree?

6. Why is a teachable spirit important? How does being teachable differ from being easily led astray?

7. What does it mean to surrender our precious opinion?

8. Discuss the following: *"Conviction without love is just an angry opinion. Conviction with love proves that what is true is also alive. That it is not only a code, but a transformative power. Conviction alone needs desperately to be proven accurate at all costs. In short, it only survives when it wins. And unfortunately for our opinion, Christ has called us to be losers."*

9. How does it affect you to know that every time you discount someone's life and worth because they disagree with your take on faith—every time you notch them downward, according to Scripture—you are spiraling yourself the same?

vanilla me   7

There it was.

Exactly where I had suspected: in the stack of clothes in Dav's closet just behind the folded brown turtleneck dickey he hated, wrapped in red and green paper with little Berts and Ernies printed all over. It was two weeks before Christmas. Dav was at a football game for the afternoon, and I had successfully hunted down and found the present he had bought me.

I was elated. This had been an ongoing pursuit of mine for years—ferreting out any of the Christmas gifts intended for me that had been hidden about the house. I anticipated the holidays with such gusto that I had spent many lazy *summer* days prescouting the house to determine what family members might consider great hiding spaces come yuletide. My strategy was that they would choose a nook or cranny that would seemingly take the most time to extricate. To this end they would never expect a seven-year-old like me to have enough time to search it out in the window of time that they could run a quick errand. What they did not foresee, however, was that

I would have already done the heavy lifting of the searching in the warm months so that in even the briefest of time windows come December, I would be able to run swiftly through my checklist of curious crevices. I had narrowed down Dav's potential hiding spaces to seven—and, lo and behold, right behind option number three, I had struck oil.

Of course, now came a more challenging conundrum. I had exhausted so much effort in strategizing the finding of the item, I had not considered what I might do with it once it was in my grasp. I hesitated to even touch it, considering the potential penalties: If I moved the gift, Dav might notice. If Dav noticed, he might tell Mom and Dad, who could potentially consider denying me Dav's present— or worse yet *all* my presents—or even worse: ban me from experiencing the holidays *in their entirety*. I pictured myself locked in my room with a math book and a number two pencil, staring at a sign reading "good children wait" while hearing the sounds of laughter and Frank Sinatra lilting gently from the living room.

Wouldn't happen.

Before I realized what I was doing, I seized the present and unwrapped it feverishly.

WHAT WAS I DOING?!

Had I gone mentally insane? I was as good as caught! I stared down at my hands as if they were coated in crystal meth. The exposed present lay there, shrapnel of colored paper strewn about like the crumbs of a stolen doughnut. I had momentarily lost myself. Ravenous like some emaciated carnivore that had eyed a crippled, motherless doe on the savannah. I had succumbed to a momentary urge of desire, and now my actions were irreversible.

Oh, well. Might as well use the sucker.

It was a book I had wanted, so I sat down on the floor of the closet with a flashlight and the door closed and read through the entire thing. Beginning to end. Completely used up the gift. Had a blast, too. It was the best book I had ever read. Well—for a seven-year-old.

And then—remorse.

I glanced about the floor of the closet and evaluated the carnage. I felt a sense of shame. Not because I was not supposed to have this object (because I was supposed to have this object)—but I was not supposed to have it *now*. I was, rather, supposed to have it *eventually*. My impatience had been a form of gluttony-turned-obesity: a need to have the whole thing this very moment instead of landing the good thing at the precise and intended perfect timing. I was deeply ashamed.

However, I was also good with scissors and tape.

I found that by trimming off the ripped edges and smoothing out the crumples, I was able to rewrap the present almost imperceptibly. I finished the job and carefully inserted the gift back behind the sweater where I had discovered it. I then gathered the remains of the paper, double-bagged it, and shoved it underneath all the garbage at the very bottom of the receptacle behind the house. The perfect crime.

When Dav arrived home, I played it cool and collected. I was both flabbergasted and impressed with myself when he emerged from his closet without the slightest inclination toward the injustice that had taken place. It suddenly dawned on me that there were some transgressions for which I might never receive a comeuppance. I lay in bed that night in the bunk underneath Dav, smiling giddily to myself as the conquering Moriarty to his baffled Sherlock. I had committed an act of treason and yet swindled myself a state of immunity. I was an ubervillain.

Until the Christmas Eve gift.

On Christmas Eve it was a tradition in our family to unwrap one (and only one) gift to play with that evening—a sort of celebratory appetizer for the buffet of gift-giving that would follow the morning after. It was also an unspoken tradition that Dav and I always chose each other's gift to open.

DAV:	You're gonna love what I got you.
ME:	*I think I'm gonna open what Brad got me instead.*
DAV:	No, you're not, stupid. We always open each other's present. Always.
ME:	*Yeah, but—you know. Don't want to get stuck in a rut. That's how addictions are formed.*
DAV:	Shut up. You're gonna open mine, and you're gonna read it, and you're gonna love it.
ME:	*Oh. Is it a book?*

So I did. I opened Dav's present as the one to tide me over all Christmas Eve night. And you have to understand that at the age of seven, we did not sleep Christmas Eve night. Did. Not. Sleep. Not even for ten minutes. We alternated playing checkers, listening to *A Charlie Brown Christmas* on LP, and staring at the ceiling all night long. All. Night. Long. The lone respite from these maddening inches toward morning was the Christmas Eve gift. Dav and I intentionally gave each other something that would while away significant hours. Three hours and seventeen minutes, to be exact. I knew this because that's how long it had taken me to read the book in Dav's closet earlier that month.

So I selected Dav's present as the one to tide me over all Christmas Eve night. But I had already opened and read that book. Dav did not know this—and I did not want him to know this. Due to the fact that we shared a bedroom and were awake all Eve, I only had one option.

Pretend to read it again in front of him.

So for the next three hours and seventeen minutes, I pretended to read Dav's gift for the very first time—wishing that it in fact *was* the very first time so I would not have to add torture upon torture— pretending upon waiting.

I could've kicked myself for being so foolish. An ounce of fore-thought would have made all the difference. I began to process this remorse in my head.

> *Why did I snoop? I knew snooping was wrong. I knew opening the present and reading the book early was wrong. I knew rewrapping it and lying about it was wrong. If I had never opened that book, I would not be bored now. I'm really paying for that mistake. I will never do that again because I hate being bored. Of course, I also wouldn't be bored right now if I had hunted down Brad's present instead of Dav's. I wonder what Brad got me. I bet he got me that other book I really wanted. Ooooh, it would be awe-some to have that book right now. Too bad I didn't ever*

find that present. Of course, I know where that present
is now. It's under the tree. I couldn't go find it now and
unwrap it and read it and wrap it back up tonight. No.
That's ridiculous. But I could. You know, I bet I could.
Yeah. I'm going to do that.

I convinced Dav of the ease in which this scenario should play out as if I did not already have documented proof of its deceptive power. I suggested that we attempt to ease open our bedroom door (our bedroom door squeaked like a condemned building—I think it was rigged this way by Dad) just a few inches and slip out, tiptoeing down the hall with a detour through the kitchen, and then entering the den from the doorway farthest from Mom and Dad's bedroom. It was fairly easy to walk without noise because we were wearing the sort of pajamas that had feet sewn into the legs. This encouraged sneaking, but also made walking the kitchen linoleum impossible without sliding a few additional unwanted yards and breaking one's ankle in half.

Dav and I shuffled inches by inches across the kitchen until our eyes were peeking through the crack in the swinging door between the refrigerator and the painting of the old man interceding over a loaf of bread. We pushed the door open just a smidge and peered in, allowing our eyes to adjust to the dark. Neither of us dared to set a foot within the perimeter of the Christmas tree, for fear that the Lord would smite us down like the unclean entering the Holy of Holies. As the light of the moon became more perceptible through the window behind the Christmas tree, we began to identify the faint outlines of what were certainly our Christmas gifts.

ME: *Do you SEE that?!*

DAV: What? See what?

ME: *That, Dav. THAT! That thing sticking up beside the tree! Is that what I think it is?!*

DAV: That's the frond of the fern plant.

ME: *Oh. I thought it was the handlebar of a Schwinn.*

DAV: Nope. Fern frond. And you didn't ask for a Schwinn.

ME: *I didn't want one when I asked for stuff, but I want one now.*

DAV: Since when?

ME: *Since I thought that fern frond was a handlebar.*

DAV: I don't see anything.

ME: *You're not really looking. You see that box-shaped thing below the tree? That's probably a television.*

DAV: That's probably a box. Like a present. A present in a box.

ME: *Not THAT box-shaped thing. THAAAAT box-shaped thing.*

DAV: That IS the television. The one we've had for five years.

ME: *And that round thing by the sofa.*

DAV: The ottoman.

ME: *That's probably Santa crouched into a ball, waiting to get us when we come in to peek at the presents.*

DAV: To get us?

ME: *With a net. Right before he shoves us in the bag.*

DAV: What do you spend your time thinking about?

But I would not have time to follow up that question with an answer, because just as we were beginning to realize our voices were rising past a whisper, we heard a distinct *squeeeak*.

The floor. In the hallway. That was a footstep. A definite footstep. Someone had heard us—or was at least suspicious—and that someone was heading our way.

We were so utterly and completely busted. Dav and I grasped one another by the shoulders, standing crouched but absolutely still, stunned like a hedgehog about to be flattened under the front left tire of an eighteen-wheeler. Our senses were suddenly heightened as we locked every muscle and stood tentatively in front of the Kenmore, waiting for another foot squeak to confirm our horror.

And then …

KRA-BASH KRA-KRONK KRA-KIPPLE KOOSH!

The icemaker in the refrigerator spilled a new tray of cubes into its plastic container a few inches from our ears. Normally this would be a mild, unnoticeable noise. But in the silence, guilt, and tension of that moment, we were convinced Christ had returned.

Dav and I scrambled and sprinted out of the kitchen, flailing spastically as we slid in our built-in-footie jammies. We flew like a terror down the hall, into our bedroom, literally slamming the door behind us—lights OFF, leaping into BED, under the COVERS, transitioning directly into fake snoring mode.

I lay there, knowing that if one of our parents stepped into our room and turned on the light, they would see my panicked chest gulping large breaths and heaving up and down under the covers. We lay there silently.

But no one ever came.

No more squeaking. No more noises of any kind. I don't know how long we waited, but not another word was spoken—and we eventually drifted off to sleep.

So close. So very close.

We had risked losing the entire jackpot—all because we simply found ourselves unable to wait. We knew good and well that our parents wanted good things for us—that they consistently gave good things to us. But even knowing the day and the hour that we would get to receive and experience those things—we were impatient. And by wanting to know—to have—to be certain of what good was coming—we almost lost it all.

EVERYTHING NOW

Certainly I have always believed the same of God. I believe that He is my Father and friend and that He loves me—that He has good things planned and intended for my life. But I would say without hesitation that the most negative Christian*ish* aspect of my own faith is that I constantly struggle with wanting it all and wanting it now.

It is the same dilemma that Jesus' closest friends faced while He walked on this earth. Jesus was friend and mentor—but in the eyes of His closest earthly companions, He was also golden promise: a promise prophesied long ago, a promise coming to life through His teachings. And though these teachings consistently and repetitively provoked those listening to live outwardly and love the person next to them, it was difficult even for the disciples to not turn this promise inward. Those closest to Christ struggled with the same question we do in this modern age: *What is in this for me and can I have it now?*

Let's be honest: Even Christ's closest followers repeatedly entreated Him with some extremely Christian*ish* questions and concerns—ones that you and I might not verbalize, but certainly dwell upon:

- Lord, first let me go and bury my father.
- Where could we get enough bread in this remote place to feed such a crowd?
- Who is the greatest in the kingdom of heaven?
- We have left everything for You. What then will there be for us?

On the surface these four sentences don't seem to have much in common with each other—that is, until you realize the sentiment behind them. The disciples' sentiment then was the same as our sentiment today. Namely: *This following-Christ thing should be benefiting me in the ways I want it to benefit me.* To make the statement that I must go bury my father before fulfilling Christ's mandate (whatever that might be) insinuates that my own order of priorities makes more sense than God's. To ask where enough bread could be gathered to feed such a crowd is to doubt that God has thought the plan all the way through (especially due to the fact that when this question was uttered, Jesus had already performed this miracle before). To ask who is the greatest in the kingdom of heaven is to slyly uncover where I personally fit within the hierarchy. To remind Jesus what I have done for Him (attached to a question of what am

I going to get back) demands payment in full for that which I have sacrificed.

Again, not sentiments we would express out loud, especially not to anyone in the church who might be listening—but sentiments that our actions certainly endorse.

For decades followers of Christ took hold of the idea that pursuing Christ was equivalent to giving things up—that in order to truly surrender to Jesus, there had to be significant denial of comfort and wealth. This shifted in the middle of the twentieth century, and a focus on prosperity became prevalent in the church. The thinking was well-intentioned: If God is a good God, then He is good all the time and He wants good things for me all the time. The challenge then became that the only ones around to define what a "good thing" was were the people themselves. And when people think "good things," people think money.

So the focus of American Christianity shifted to an age of prosperity, of wanting more and more in the name of Jesus. It was a proving of one's faith through one's bank balance—the reasoning being that affluence should bring influence. We believed that those who did not follow Christ would switch teams once they saw us happy and fat. American Christians became convinced that God wanted good things for them, and that a good thing could only mean a sudden, inexplicable fat check.

Well—it didn't quite work out.

Thousands of Christians made atrocious financial decisions on the basis of a supernatural yearning. They bought big before the blessing—and when their irrational wants were not met, they became disillusioned with God. They began to question whether or not God really did want good things for them, and therefore questioned whether or not He really is a good God. This was, of course, hogwash. God was never the one who told them they should be rich in the first place. He certainly never told them to make large purchases with money that they did not yet have. That is, rather, what they told themselves. God never even called money a good thing. He says He will give us life more abundantly, but that doesn't have anything to do with our cache of stuff. God says in fact that we worry far too much about how we will eat or what clothes we will wear. He intends to feed us and clothe us—because there are more important things begging for our attention.

So the postmodern set may feel that they dodged this bullet, never giving in to the age of church greed. In fact the "God greed" mind-set probably turned many of the postmodern generation away from the church. The funny thing is, once they distanced themselves from the church as a corporate body, they took on the same attitude—the same greed perspective—but in a different way.

A new generation may not be hooked on things, but they are addicted to another sort of greed: the greed of getting the credit. We live in a famous society, where seemingly everyone gets a shot at being a star. It is such a prevalent sentiment in society that it has bled over to the community of faith. No longer is the feeling "If I'm going to live this way for Christ, I want to be rich." Now the sentiment is "If I'm going to live this way for Christ, I want everyone to notice. I want to be esteemed and praised. I want to receive the credit." Whichever generation we come from, we have found a unique way to make Christ's sacrifice all about us.

We may not be looking for the cash-in, but we continue to live out our faith in a manner that is looking for the angle. We want to know: What is this going to do for me? If I am going to sacrifice, what is the yin to that yang? What will be my reward? If I live a lifetime of giving, will I then live an afterlifetime of getting? We look at the Beatitudes and determine which "blesseds" we're going to live out based on the perceived cash value of exactly what each inherits. We live in a materialistic culture and we assume that just because we do some selfless acts in the name of Jesus, that culture doesn't have any effect on us—but it most certainly does. We grow up being rewarded for memorizing Bible verses and receiving gold stars for Sunday school attendance and are surprised when mature faith is not an exercise in tit-for-tat prizewinning. To this end there are a whole lot of disillusioned Christians out there who are more than a smidge ticked that their walk of faith is more difficult than expected.

OBESE FOR JESUS

The saddest thought of all is that there actually *are* benefits to our faith—benefits significantly larger than the sacrifice—but we cannot recognize them because they are not the benefits for which we were longing.

Jesus called this losing our salt.

The world calls it vanilla.

I call it fat.

As a Christian culture we have grown morbidly obese: craving little pleasures, paybacks, and accolades to our heroic emotional efforts. Wanting recompense or fame and wanting it now in the way that we define. When we do not receive this desired prize, we usually buy, borrow, or take it anyway—because we decided a long time ago that we deserve it. In so doing, we take what does not belong to us, and then blame God that it didn't make us feel any better.

This flab has transformed us into unwieldy faith potatoes, all visible definition of our muscle gone to goo. So though we may feel we continue to follow Jesus deep down inside, no one on the outside can actually see even a small flicker of passion buried beneath our lazy love handles.

To this end we have begrudged and distanced ourselves. From God. From faith. From one another. And as we do, the Enemy wins. Because he has been able to distract us away from the very core idea of following Jesus: that we only truly gain when gain is not what we are after, and we only find answers for ourselves when we are being the answers for someone else.

The enemy's biggest plan for each of us is to get us navel-gazing our way through faith. If we're going to follow Jesus, the enemy wants us to follow blindly. Jesus wants us to follow with our eyes wide open and our ears alert to what we discover along the path to Him—but this is impossible when we are constantly distracted by the bonuses.

Have you ever been driving a car for a long period of time, and then suddenly realized that you don't remember the last twenty miles? You zoned out, but you kept driving because your brain has a Pavlovian response to being in that driver's seat. This is how many mistakenly believe their faith journey is supposed to look. That we surrender the directions and zone out for the ride. But Christ has a different perspective. He doesn't simply want each of us to reach the final destination in one piece. He wants us to have grown on the journey—to have conquered obstacles and discovered truths and become more like Him so that the destination means more. We cannot grow on a journey that we zone out to travel. We cannot become more Christlike by following Him while staring eternally internal. We only become more like Christ when we intentionally resist the temptation to dwell on what is in it for ourselves. We overcome obstacles when we deny this stumbling block and instead focus on the world around us.

This thought was very important to Jesus, and He clearly foresaw a day when we would be required to resist getting bland and fat—of the spice of our lives turning vanilla. He put it this way:

> *You are the salt of the earth. But if the salt loses its saltiness, how can it be made salty again? It is no longer good for anything, except to be thrown out and trampled by men. You are the light of the world. A city on a hill cannot be hidden. Neither do people light a lamp and put it under a bowl. Instead they put it on its stand, and it gives light to everyone in the house. In the same way, let your light shine before men, that they may see your good deeds and praise your Father in heaven.*
>
> Matthew 5:13–16

We aren't the salt until Christ is active in our lives and we are spreading His truth throughout mankind. *That's* the salt. But Jesus makes it a point here that even those who are living this way run the risk of *losing* this salt. That the brightest of examples could potentially have their light snuffed. Just like muscle can easily turn to fat and tasty morsels can spoil. We have to work at this faith thing—and by work I don't mean earn our salvation. I mean, rather, that we have to work at not getting lazy. We have to resist the ongoing temptation that this is about us. And we can only overcome this stumbling block when we refuse to embrace the emotion of "I deserve."

"I deserve" is the modern American mantra.

"I deserve" is rapidly sneaking into the culture of the Christian church.

"I deserve" is the enemy of everything God is trying to do in each of our lives.

The truth is, in its rawest form the heart of Christ's salvation is that it is absolutely, inarguably *not* deserved. We did not deserve rescue and Christ did not deserve to take the brunt of our sins. But He did—and therefore we are saved. From that moment on we lost every right to argue what we deserve. What we gained was the possibility and the opportunity to help someone else receive the true life that he or she also has not deserved. It is a miracle beyond description.

But in order to become the sort of true selflessness that Christ is talking about—to regain our saltiness—we've got to give up some serious creature comforts.

We've got to give up our perceived right to have whatever we want. We must give up our expectation that the Christian life should run smoothly. We must drop our indignation when the best is not delivered to our doorsteps. We must be content with less—and even take joy in having to work more for it.

Our expectation for more should be more of Christ—more of His fruit in our lives—more love for the purpose of showering that love on those within our vicinity. More patience for His mystery being revealed over a lifetime. More peace with our occupation, financial constraints, and social status. More joy in times of trial. More kindness when we are being treated antagonistically. More long-suffering when times are hard and the people around us need to hear more than just complaining. More self-control when we want, want, want and the world tells us we deserve.

We should be asking God for more open doors to reveal His love—and more sympathy and understanding for others when those doors inevitably open.

I'm certain that the life I have just described brings a certain level of stress and bile to the surface. If it does, that should reveal how much our comfort has replaced our mission in this Christian life. Because the truth is, when the characteristics listed in the previous two paragraphs are truly put into action as described, that is when life suddenly feels rewarding. Those are the scenarios where true meaning and fulfillment come. The very happiness we were trying to purchase or pray into our bank account suddenly comes through extremely different means—extremely different, but extremely real.

For all of us the action of following Christ must eventually leave the world of "what am I going to get out of this" and permanently transition into the world of "how am I going to give through this."

It is an uncomfortable transition—and one that requires resisting the temptation to hunt down and open the Christmas presents early. It is an approach that gets us off of our butts and works off the fat so that the muscles of our faith can realize definition. When all is said and done, it is the only authentic way to live. It is the discovery of every emotion we have been trying our best to purchase. And it is the only way to regain the salt to what has become a spiritually blah and vanilla me.

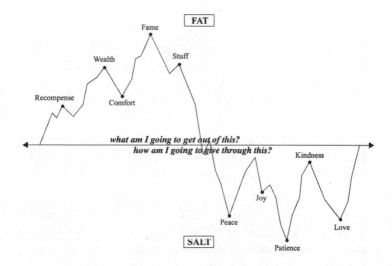

1.   In regard to your Christian faith, do you struggle with wanting it all and wanting it now?

2.Which camp do you fall into: Do you believe Christianity is about giving up things, or about prosperity?

3.   What are some of the downsides to American Christianity focusing upon prosperity?

4.   Have you ever personally experienced the following sentiment: "If I'm going to live this way for Christ, I want everyone to notice. I want to be esteemed and praised. I want to receive the credit"?

5.   Do you find yourself disillusioned with faith— struggling to see its benefits? Could this be because you are looking for the wrong benefits?

6.   In the kingdom of Christ, we only truly gain when gain is not what we are after, and we only find answers for ourselves when we are being the answers for someone else. How do we live this out?

7.   Have you ever zoned out on your Christian journey? Simply going through the learned motions without any real growth?

8.   What does it look like to work at not getting lazy in our faith?

upside is a downside 8

Why is there a part of me that takes pleasure in seeing people fail?

I don't *like* that I like to see people fail. I don't actually *want* them to fail—but every time someone else stumbles down the popularity poll, I have to gulp more than a few endorphins back down. It's not an intentional reaction. I wish those people no ill will, but something inherent in me gets a kick out of it before I realize what is happening and kick that something back where it came from.

Certainly this stems from the fact that I am acutely aware of every instance I myself make a mistake; every time I do wrong, I feel myself slipping rapidly down the chutes that took eleven or twelve ladders to climb up. I don't want other people to fail, but I know that I fail and I occasionally want some company way down in those dumps. The lower everyone else is, the less space I have between us to climb.

Hence, those pesky endorphins.

Consequently I was elated when the headmaster announced to my third-grade class at Gate Fellowship Christian School that

Halloween would be a theme costume day and that the best costume in the school would win a prize. This thrilled me for a number of reasons:

1.   Simply acknowledging Halloween at a Christian school chapel was akin to granting us permission to watch *The Smurfs*.

2.   Most of our school competitions involved physical agility, of which I was in short supply. This competition was purely creative. Bring it on.

3.   The competition was not only for the second grade. It was between all grades—an opportunity for me to knock the business out of some high schoolers that, quite honestly, were a little too comfortable with their perception that they were running the place.

4.   The theme for the competition was "storybook."

"Storybook" was a fairly edgy theme for a Christian costume competition, especially one already tainted with the stain of Halloween. The three previous themes had been "Bible characters," "characters found within the Bible," and "characters from books (suggested option: the Bible)." I shouldn't have been completely shocked we were now branching out into literature. After all, you can only milk the teat of biblical characters so many times before you have to start dressing in a single fig leaf or arrive decked out as one of the descriptions in Song of Solomon.

Halloween was always tricky in the evangelical world. You didn't want to give the impression you were celebrating Satan's day, but you also didn't want sinner kids bragging about having the most candy. Christian schools and churches tended to meet somewhere in the middle, celebrating "autumn" instead of "Halloween" and just happening to celebrate it at dusk on October 31. This is why most of my childhood Halloweens were spent at "fall festivals," where witches and goblins were replaced with hayrides and cakewalks. It was a nice swap. You can't exactly put icing and sprinkles on a goblin.

As soon as I arrived home, I slammed my bedroom door behind me and pulled out a clean notepad and my number two pencil. It was time to design my masterpiece. I first considered my resources. My budget: none. My available materials: whatever was in my closet. I went straight to the bookshelf for inspiration.

For an eight-year-old the bookcase in my room was fairly overcrowded because of my love for reading. I perused the options:

- Narnia. Seemed complicated. If I went as one of the Pevensie children, I would have to dress in the clothing of a British prep school, which was basically what I had to wear to school every day already. No one would notice. On the other hand, if I went as Aslan, there would be a great deal of itching.
- The Laura Ingalls Wilder *Little House* series. No way. I had to suffer through the Michael Landon TV show every Monday night as it was. Besides, I looked good in neither plaid nor calico. They weren't slimming.
- Charlie Brown. Wow—shaving my head. That would get some serious attention. Would Mom allow me to ruin my yellow IZOD shirt by drawing that one thick jagged line on it with a permanent marker? I'd have to think about that one.

- *Robinson Crusoe.* I couldn't even remember what happened in that book. I opened it up to remind myself, only to discover that I had never read it and that this particular copy had been overdue from a library in another city for three years. Oops. This made me feel guilty, so I buried the book amid all the toys and dirty clothes underneath my bed.
- Charles Dickens' *A Christmas Carol.* This always felt like more of a Halloween story to me than a Christmas story, plus I was afraid I would get docked points for associating with ghosts. Also, chains are heavy.
- *Foxe's Book of Martyrs.* Perhaps a tad intense.

Hmm. My first consideration in this sort of endeavor was that I did not want to dress up as a character that anyone else would select. The second consideration was that I wanted a potentially winning costume that would require the least amount of effort. I stared into my closet: four baseball caps and some old jeans with patches on the knees, a pair of brown slacks, and about a hundred white T-shirts. I ventured down the hall into the coat closet and dug all the way into the back. There was an oversize plaid winter coat that, on someone my size, would cover my body down to my ankles. The wheels began to turn. The next thing I knew, I was sticking one baseball cap inside another with their bills facing opposing directions. I cut up a paper grocery sack and covered the two baseball caps with the brown paper. I put on the plaid coat and my brown slacks. I dug through the toy box and found an old bubble-soap pipe. My ensemble was complete.

I was Sherlock Holmes.

I took great pride in the fact that I came up with the idea and constructed the costume myself. I was also pleased with the fact that it only took me twelve minutes to do so. The outfit was not cumbersome or uncomfortable and indulged me the sensation of slight rebellion because my mouth held a device used for smoking all day long. Thanks, Sir Arthur Conan Doyle. You're the shizzle.

The morning came and it was only at the very moment itself that I realized I would be walking the mile to school along busy roadways, dressed like a smoking British sleuth. Neat. I threw my backpack on over the thick coat and drudged on through the seventy-degree, late-October Georgia morning. When I finally arrived at school, I combed the hallways to make certain there was no other Holmeses in the sea of familiar storybook faces. There was Holly Hobbie with her oversized bonnet and freakish beady black eyes. A couple of flying monkeys from *The Wizard of Oz*. Raggedy Ann and Raggedy Andy. A fellow dressed up like Moses (somebody missed a memo). Tollie Ayscue was Sir Lancelot—and Mark Lind, who always walked to the beat of a different drummer, was some sort of Vulcan.

ME: Are you Spock from Star Trek?

MARK: You wish. I am a superior Vulcan. One who does not debase himself by associating with humans.

ME: *Is that in a book?*

MARK: It is in my mind.

ME: *You know we're supposed to dress like somebody from a book.*

MARK: Rules are for the narrow-minded.

ME: *You're really weird.*

MARK: You're the one wearing two baseball caps.

The coolest guy in high school (Jerry) and his cronies were dressed up like S. E. Hinton's *The Outsiders*, but personally I just thought they looked like a bunch of Fonzies and Chachis. Jerry waved me over to where he and his buddies were sitting in the bed of his gray Ford pickup. For a moment I thought I was going to get smacked for some absurd reason. You never knew why the upperclassmen would smack you. Perhaps it was because I had cut up a grocery sack from his favorite store to make the hat. Perhaps he just hated the British. Maybe he thought that my bubble pipe was making fun of his two-packs-a-day habit. All I knew is that I did not want to approach his truck. But he was laughing. An inviting laugh. A "you're-one-of-us-now" laugh. I knew my costume was better than everyone else's, but I hadn't realized it held this sort of power over upperclassmen. I approached.

JERRY: What's up, Steele?
ME: *My mame's Mark.*
JERRY: Your mame?
ME: *Name. Sorry. Name. My name is Nark.*
JERRY: Nice to know, Nark. Your name's also Steele.
ME: *Yeah, but—you know. I thought maybe you had it backwards. Because of all the smoking and what that does to the brain.*
JERRY: Geez Louise, Steele.
ME: *Mark.*
JERRY: Did you know that the winner today is the guy who gets the most applause?

ME: *What do you mean?*

JERRY: At assembly at the end of the day. They're choosing
           which costume is best by which costume gets the
           most applause.

ME: *I did not know that.*

JERRY: Me and my buddies just want you to know that
           we're gonna be cheering for you.

ME: *Wha—huh?*

JERRY: We want you to win.

I suddenly had a warm feeling that was 49 percent gratitude, 50 percent fear, and 1 percent thick coat. This sentiment should have elated me, but I was too confused to feel any sort of semblance of thanks.

ME: *Wha—why?*

JERRY: Huh?

ME: *Why would you help me win?*

JERRY: Do we need a reason? We're sitting here, watching
           everybody, thinking "Who's done the best job,"
           and then we see you, Steele.

ME: *Mark.*

JERRY: And I think, that's pretty good. That is a pretty
           good Bigfoot.

ME: *I'm Sherlock Holmes.*

JERRY: Even better.

ME: *Bigfoot's not in a book.*

JERRY: See you at two, kid.

I wandered to my homeroom in a bit of a stupor. I suddenly had moral support. Me. The guy who didn't win student body president last month, even though my presentation included puppets and an awesome rewrite of the theme to *Good Times*. Mark Steele had the upperclassmen in his pocket. Come two o'clock today, this was one Christian school that was going to have some awfully disappointed flying monkeys.

As I strutted past the lockers, I got a better view of Raggedy Ann and Raggedy Andy. The look of them gave me a moment of pause. Legitimate yarn. They had used actual yarn for the hair. And through all that makeup, I could barely tell who was underneath.

Until I saw the tears.

It was Carol and Shelly. Two best-friend upperclassmen. Carol was emotionally devastated over something, her tears beginning to drip red clown makeup onto her white apron smock. I had never really spoken to Carol, but knew her well because every time I caught her making out with her boyfriend, I would raise my eyebrows like Groucho Marx, ribbing "wubba wubba." Shelly, as Raggedy Andy, was consoling her and urging her to get to class. They each saw me out of a corner of an eye and moved along. Though I should have felt at least a morsel of sympathy, I found myself instead dreading the juggernaut one-two punch of real yarn and actual tears. Talk about a winning combination. I had quite the battle ahead of me.

The first round of competition was within each separate class-room. My class of forty-two students encompassed both third and fourth grade, so I would have my work cut out for me. All par-ticipating students were asked to stand and march around the room like runway models. The kid with the wealthiest dad had dressed up like the Gingerbread Man, but to the glee of absolutely everyone, his elaborate and complicated headdress had burst into pieces of Styrofoam when he attempted to squeeze his costumed noggin through the doorjamb. He sobbed long and hard about never winning anything, but we all knew he had already won the jackpot of rich parents, so we moved on pretty quickly.

I heaved a sigh of relief. This didn't leave any real competition unless you included Vulcan Mark, who was furious he was disqualified for not proving his character was inside any form of written word. I quickly shot him the Vulcan sign. He showed me his hand as well, though his fingers were arranged in a slightly different fashion.

I was crowned the costume king of my classroom, which automatically fast-passed me to the stage at assembly. Once there I would stand alongside eight other classroom winners, judged by our peers to determine who was truly the brightest and cleverest of all underage Georgians (at least that's what I believed it would mean).

As I boldly marched toward assembly, followed by my young entourage of onlookers, my confidence grew. I could not remember ever having a day when so many other people paled next to me. It was a luscious feeling. I suckled it and quickly craved that all future days would hold this same sort of elation. And then I saw him.

Another Sherlock Holmes.

In fact, a significantly better Sherlock Holmes. One of the high schoolers had chosen the exact same storybook character. The hat appeared authentic. He held a magnifying glass. *OF COURSE! A magnifying glass!* His clothing insinuated the accurate time period. I gazed. I coveted. I nodded.

ME: *Hey.*

SHERLOCK: Hey, Steele.

ME: *Did you win in your classroom?*

SHERLOCK: Nope. Why? Did you?

ME: *Uh—yeah.*

SHERLOCK Really? Funny. My costume's better than yours.

ME: *I know. Who beat you?*

SHERLOCK: Raggedy Ann and Andy.

ME: *Raggedy—you mean Carol and Shelly?*

SHERLOCK: Yeah. Jerry really wanted them to win, so he got
              everybody cheering for them. Didn't really stand
              a chance.

ME: *Jerry? Ford Pickup Jerry? Smack-a-third-grader*
              Jerry?

SHERLOCK: Yup. Carol didn't seem very happy about it,
              though. Oh well. Good luck, Holmes.

And the sleuth was gone. A cold sweat began trickling down my forehead. What had happened? Had I done something to unknowingly disenfranchise the brutes of the senior class? Had I, in my cocksureness, turned their affection against me and toward sad girls with authentic yarn? I stared at my costume in the reflection of the better Sherlock's locker door. Surely the other students saw what I saw: superiority, craftsmanship, and dare I say, a dapper fellow.

But no freaking magnifying glass.

Oh, well. What was done was done. I made my way to assembly—and stepped up onto the stage.

It didn't take long before seven of the competitors were eliminated due to lack of applause. *Go ahead, kindergarteners. Scream all you want for your little Curious George. You are no match for my bubble pipe.* Eventually it came down to two finalists. On one side of the stage: myself, cocking my eyebrows and speaking in a bad British accent. On the other side: Raggedy Ann and Andy, Ann's makeup smeared so much from crying that she slightly resembled Gene Simmons. It was the moment of truth.

I looked out into the crowd. I saw Jerry and his cohorts ready to pop out of their seats in applause, and I knew that he had changed his mind. He must have seen Carol's tears and, in a moment of class unity, decided to support her instead of his favorite Li'l Sherlock. I closed my eyes as the judge placed his hand over the impressive yarn atop Carol and Shelly's heads.

Just a smattering of applause. Hardly any noise at all. I couldn't believe it.

And even though there were tears running down Carol's (and now Shelly's) face, I could not help but feel a surge of elation throughout my body. These people loved me. They really loved me. I was slightly sorry that meant others had to be loved less, but so be it. Somebody's got to win in life and it only makes sense that somebody should be me. I awaited the deluge. The judge's hand was placed over my head ...

Jerry leapt to his feet, as did every bully that owed him. They cheered loudly and long—and most in the school followed suit.

The judge declared me the winner and handed me the trophy. I stared out into the small sea of faces, overwhelmed that I had been appreciated for my costume cleverness. It was a skill I always knew I had, but had never considered I would have to wait this long to have it applauded publicly. I looked out at Jerry to wave thank you.

But Jerry was not looking my direction.

He was shouting "yeah!" over and over.

But he was shouting it toward Carol.

About me, but toward Carol.

I was puzzled.

The look on his face was venomous, practically evil. I glanced at Carol as her tears turned to sobs and she ran from the stage and out the door.

The bell rang.

I began walking home: a mini-Brit sleuth with a pipe in mouth and trophy in hand. Gray clouds had rolled in and the weather was beginning to transition to November cold. A Ford pickup suddenly swerved in front of me, kicking up dust.

JERRY:	Way to go, killer.
ME:	*Sherlock's not the killer. Sherlock catches the killer.*
JERRY:	Whatever, nerd.
ME:	*I take it you're not familiar with the book.*
JERRY:	I only let winners ride in my truck. You wanna ride home, winner?
ME:	*Sure.*

I rode in the back, clutching my trophy and my backpack beside four tenth-graders, and thrilled that I was wearing a heavy coat. The tenth-graders stared at me, clearly wishing that, just once, Jerry would call them *winner*. The next thing I knew, Jerry was pulling into my driveway.

JERRY: There you go, Steele.

ME: *Thanks.*

JERRY: Don't look so depressed. You just won the contest.

ME: *Yeah—*

I hesitated. Uncertain if I should test the waters.

ME: *But I hated to beat Carol. She seemed so sad.*

Jerry spit out an expletive and called Carol a word I wouldn't repeat for several more years.

JERRY: Forget her. She got exactly what she deserved.

With that, Jerry's gray Ford pickup peeled out of the driveway. The same Ford pickup I had seen Carol making out inside time upon time. I watched as the truck disappeared around the horizon. I wandered inside to where my oldest brother, Brad, was watching *Gilligan's Island.*

BRAD: Jerry brought you home?

ME: *Yup.*

BRAD: Did he say anything about why he broke up with Carol last night?

ME: *He broke up with Carol—last night?*

BRAD: Well—no duh, Sherlock.

I had felt so good in spite of others feeling so bad. Concerned only for the manner in which I was being raised up, disregarding completely the backs upon which my height was enabled. I continually denied the reality I was witnessing firsthand. I had seen others crumbling with my own eyes and had done nothing about it because there was a chance their misfortune would bring me what I wanted. I received exactly what I had pursued: the win. But it felt much more like a loss, because the manner in which I had won proved only that I had been a pawn in a more nefarious game, one in which I played ignorant and therefore became the fool.

I would like to say that my actions that day were very unhuman.

But the truth is, they were human. Very, very human.

That is precisely the problem.

UNHUMANLY POSSIBLE

There is a sinful nature in every single one of us and, left unaddressed to fester and exponentially grow, it will slowly overtake all of our best intentions.

It is human to live selfishly, to have a continual radar up searching for the means to get ahead and rise to the top. Ignoring the plight of the neighbor. Continually neglecting to notice the poverty and pain across the world that empowers our own wealth and comfort. These are human sentiments. Human traits. It is the expected result of the decision of a person to abandon another for personal gain.

If you want to see someone act unhuman, you'd have to take a look at Jesus.

Jesus loved in a way that you and I could never imagine. Yes, we've heard over and over again how He sacrificed His life so that all may come to God—but it goes even deeper than that. You and I have a capacity to love. That capacity broadens as we abandon our selfishness and risk for others. How do we risk? We allow ourselves to be vulnerable to the point of need. We love so deeply and surrender so mutually that we become a necessity to the person we are loving and they in turn become a necessity to us.

But with Christ the measure was out of balance. He loved us, truly and deeply loved us—but He did not need us. He couldn't. There was not a hole in Jesus waiting to be filled. To this end Jesus had to become the only necessary love within the exchange. The only sacrifice. His life, death, and sacrifice were unbelievably one-sided. A shocking act of selflessness. There was literally nothing in it for Jesus, with the exception of His affection for mankind. He was fully human and yet decided of His own accord to reject selfishness wholly: an entirely unhuman thing to do. Because Jesus was willing to respond unhumanly in His humanity, you and I were rescued.

That's the upside.

But there's a downside to the upside.

He is expecting you and me to get unhuman too.

There it is. That's the nutshell. There were a thousand evidences that Jesus was the Savior—the Son of God—but the most noticeable one was that He was willing to love in ways humans did not choose to love. He was selfless even though humans were selfish. He gave to those who did not earn. He did not crush others to get to the top.

He spent time with the outcasts. He healed the sick. He showed affection to the unlovable. He turned the other cheek. He did not get even. He did not prove Himself right. He did not belligerently argue His point. He did not boycott and criticize. He loved. It was unusual and it certainly drew the crowds. It ministered in a more infective way than any ministry before or since. He loved extravagantly and famously. He loved many and often. Word spread like wildfire.

And then He told us to go and do the same.

The problem with the modern church is that we're trying to love, but we're doing it on the sliding scale of America. In other words, we are limiting our love to a small circle within manageable limits that potentially could range between our weekly tithers to neighborhoods in our local community. An occasional mission trip fits in there as well. The actual plight of the world as it suffers from our decisions and repercussions doesn't seem to play a regular role. And the most significant crime is that if we are involved in enough love-themed outreaches, we don't keep our personal interactions in much check at all. In our daily life we continue to judge, to spread rumors, to condescend. We continue to roll our eyes at those whose ways differ. Even as Christians we harbor distrust and resentment in our hearts toward interest groups, political parties, and *(gulp)* sometimes other races. And we feel so correct that it doesn't even cross our minds that we are unloving.

As a modern church we have become extremely antagonistic toward those in the world who don't already match our demographic. We gaze at their lives and our eyes rapidly drift first to the core sins. We itemize those sins and determine that there will be no love given until there is first restitution.

Even though Christ did not require restitution from us.

Instead He was the restitution for us.

First.

Before we did anything.

And yet for some reason we live for justice.

We want comeuppance.

Again, this is human.

However …

The first time someone came to this world as a human and loved in a way that was unhuman, it changed everything. What would happen if, in His name, the rest of us followed suit?

It's not a shocking thought. Jesus laid out the plan while He was still here:

> *But I tell you who hear me: Love your enemies, do good to those who hate you, bless those who curse you, pray for those who mistreat you. If someone strikes you on one cheek, turn to him the other also. If someone takes your cloak, do not stop him from taking your tunic. Give to everyone who asks you, and if anyone takes what belongs to you, do not demand it back. Do to others as you would have them do to you.*
>
> Luke 6:27–31

That's just crazy talk! Why on earth would I be a stepstool for someone who wishes me ill? Why would I be the first to love when I have no proof that I'm going to receive any affection back? Why would I not talk back—not hate back—not HIT back? Why would

I bless the cursers and give a one-way sign while the other guy is flipping the bird? I don't get it. I just don't get it. And that is exactly the point. No one gets it. Because it is love. It is not the natural response of a human. It is instead the natural response of God. And for a human to deliver on those levels with nothing promised in return? Why—it is the most tangible proof on this touch-it/feel-it planet that God is real and that God is, indeed, love.

> *If you love those who love you, what credit is that to you? Even "sinners" love those who love them. And if you do good to those who are good to you, what credit is that to you? Even "sinners" do that. And if you lend to those from whom you expect repayment, what credit is that to you? Even "sinners" lend to "sinners," expecting to be repaid in full. But love your enemies, do good to them, and lend to them without expecting to get anything back. Then your reward will be great, and you will be sons of the Most High, because he is kind to the ungrateful and wicked. Be merciful, just as your Father is merciful.*
>
> Luke 6:32–36

Boy, Jesus is just not going to make this easy, is He?

And yet it really does make perfect sense.

Christ had nothing to gain and everything to lose by loving us unconditionally. He did all the painful work while leaving the gate open for you and me to casually walk away from His love. It is exactly why it worked. His sacrifice broke sin and death and destroyed their power. But that love has got to be carried on. And the only ones around to do it are you and me. The Christians. It is the very thing that makes us "little Christs."

If we can somehow come to the point of shutting down the selfishness—choosing to guard our hearts consistently through our days so that our wants do not win—then the world just might see Jesus again. The real Jesus. Not just Christians.

And, if we can reach this level of love, there actually is a payoff, even for us. However, it is a payoff worth much more than that which we were previously pursuing:

> *Do not judge, and you will not be judged. Do not condemn, and you will not be condemned. Forgive, and you will be forgiven. Give, and it will be given to you. A good measure, pressed down, shaken together and running over, will be poured into your lap. For with the measure you use, it will be measured to you.*
>
> Luke 6:37–38

Everything we were grabbing for, we are to instead give. It is the only way to truly seize it. Even after we choose to follow Jesus, we each continue to stuff an emptiness. This emptiness is meant to be filled to overflowing with love for others, but we have instead attempted to plug it with aspirations. Accolades that puff ourselves up—even at the expense of those we stand upon.

This attempt is all too human.

And that is exactly why it is time for it to end.

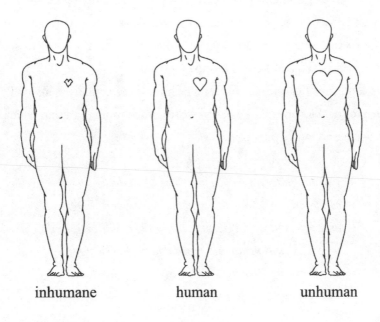

inhumane   human   unhuman

1.   Are there ways in modern culture where we benefit (even unknowingly) from the suffering of others? Discuss how this might be possible.

2.   What about the issue of ignorance? What results from our ignorance of current injustices within our world and community? What is our Christian responsibility?

3.   Be introspective for a moment. In what ways do you live selfishly?

4.   What does it mean to "love your neighbor as yourself"? How is this possible if you are unaware of their hurts and challenges?

5.   Why do we resist getting involved with the pain of others?

6.   If selfishness is very human, what would it look like in practice to live "unhuman"?

7.   What does it mean to say *"the modern church is trying to love, but we're doing it on the sliding scale of America"*?

8.   What would unconditional, Jesus-reflecting love truly look like in our modern culture? In your daily life and community?

the grace discount 9

The mustard color that coated the top 50 percent of the school van would not have been such an eyesore if the bottom half had not been the shade of a Snickers bar left out in the sun too long. It was (and I believe even listed in the Blue Book as such) the ugliest vehicle allowed to be driven on public roads in the twentieth century. But, as well as a monstrosity for the eyes, it also enjoyed the bonus of being a death trap on wheels. People who drove directly behind us risked dying of secondhand smoke, if they were not first bludgeoned to death by the flying detached tailpipe.

The van belonged to the church and school and, as such, had large cursive writing emblazoned on the side (mostly on the aged chocolate half): *Christian Center Academy*. It was a motion billboard advertising that we believed in Jesus and hoped you would follow the van to Him. At least it would have advertised this, had the goings-on inside the van been slightly more Christian.

I was thirteen and my older brothers were fifteen and seventeen. We were Christians, but we were also morons celebrating puberty. As my mother was the head (and only) teacher, the van was our family's to use as we pleased. Having free rein to a van did not assist in our accountability.

The van was disintegrating. Vans do this when they turn eighty. We were always suspicious that the van was actually the very first car ever built. Perhaps it was a Model T with some new aluminum siding thrown up to disguise it. If there were any seat belts in the van, they were lost forever in the abyss between the cushions where we had also lost four bags of Cheetos, two library books, and a nearsighted second-grader. The shocks were almost completely destroyed. This was more than likely due to the fact that on several occasions we would stand in the back of the van as it was driving down the highway and physically jump up and down or rock it side to side so that it looked like the house party in *Electric Boogaloo*. This would cause small parts of the van to dislodge themselves from the undercarriage and bobble away forever on the highway. If you've ever swerved to avert a significant metal object in the middle of an interstate lane, it used to belong to us.

The reason we knew the van was a death trap was because the engine was not under the hood. No. The engineers of this particular mobile fiasco considered it a much more clever idea to strategically place the engine inside the van itself under a thin plastic cover between the driver and the passenger in the front seat. This occasion-ally came in handy, because you could physically unlatch the plastic and expose the running engine right next to you while driving. We did this often. It just seemed like a cool and dangerous thing to do. It was also how we restarted the van every time it stalled in the middle

of a well-traveled road. The van would sputter and conk out completely at the most inopportune moments. I don't know exactly how
we came to this conclusion, but for some reason it became clear that
the way to fix it was to open up the air filter and allow some oxygen
into the carburetor. We would do this—in the middle of the road,
mind you—by uncovering the engine inside the van, uncovering the
air filter, and then shoving a pencil into the carburetor valve.

Seriously.

We shoved a small, sharp writing utensil into the carburetor
valve to let the air in.

In the middle of the road.

And then the van would start.

A lot of parents must have been praying for us during this season
of our lives.

Inside that van we had way too much freedom. For fleeting
moments we felt like we owned the world. As if we could drive off
the edge of the planet and drift away into the atmosphere. It was our
little cubicle of rowdiness—driving to and fro across Atlanta city
limits, celebrating our little bacchanalia of adolescence and consistently forgetting what was advertised on the outside of the van.

One afternoon, while driving across town to see *Red Dawn*, our
very first PG-13 movie (a rating that made us feel like we were view-
ing something sort of dirty), our best friend Ronnie had a wild-hair,
out-of-nowhere idea—and for literally no reason whatsoever, stuck his
naked assets out of the front window and began mooning every car
in sight. In a city as large as Atlanta, you would expect that the only
observers would be strangers. Unfortunately the driver to Ronnie's
immediate right was the most conservative parent in our school.

That didn't go over so well.

We were suddenly given more restrictions regarding our previous van freedoms. We were no longer allowed to tote girls hither and thither—no longer allowed to drive anywhere we wanted anytime we wanted. No longer permitted to blare Twisted Sister and Quiet Riot from 96 Rock out the open windows. No longer allowed to do doughnuts in the Kroger parking lot. We had never technically been permitted to do any of these things, but it seemed to us that if we had not been told to *not* do them, we were good to go. To this end the list of things forbidden inside the church billboard van was finally clarified:

- No secular music
- No unauthorized girls
- No jumping out of seats
- No nudity of any kind

We really had been obedient for the most part. Seriously. Once we were out of sight of the parents, it was simply too easy to forget that the words on the outside of the van were continuing to hold us accountable on its inside. We daily got away with way too much because we were lovable and because we were just obedient enough to not be identified as backsliders or rebel kids. We rode a fine line between just-good-enough-to-avoid-punishment and just-bad-enough-to-have-fun. I suppose you could say that we collected grace from our parents in our home hours and then wasted that grace whenever away.

One very chilly October morning, Dav and I were required to head outside and start up the van. Brad, who was the actual expert at the insert-a-writing-tool-into-the-carburetor approach to driving, was elsewhere. This built inside Dav and me a fifty-fifty split of excitement and trepidation. Many times the van's ignition would start of its own accord. Certainly this frigid morn would be one of those times.

We opened the front door, which in icy weather was a two-man job. We were required to squeeze the handle together with at least three fists while bracing against the side of the van with one's right foot. We used to pour lukewarm water on all the icy spots—until it made the windshield crack. We pushed hard until we heard the everyday *KER-CLUNK* of the door opening, wondering whether the sound was ice, eroding metal, or chipping paint, only to discover that we did not care. The door finally opened.

Dav turned the ignition.

Nothing. Silence. Not even the initial *ch* of a *chuggachugga*.

We suddenly realized that we were elated. Dav and I had never been given the opportunity to jimmy-rig the van engine before. We had seen this simple trick accomplished many times, but it had always been verboten for us—the younger teens. Dav began to unlatch the engine cover while I was sent to locate and fetch a pencil.

You would think that in any American home, a pencil would be handy, but at the Steeles' on a school morning, I might as well have been searching for the body of Jimmy Hoffa—and he probably wouldn't have had a pencil either. Dav was calling out for me to hurry. He was freezing. I opened another drawer; no pencil. I began to panic. *Did no one in this house use graphite to write anything down anymore?! When I don't have an urgent need for one, this house is practically a festival of pencils! But now that I actually have need, they've all vanished down the vortex of a collapsed dying star.* I began to feel anger toward all writing utensils, and thus abandoned my search.

I improvised. I grabbed the first similar-sized item I laid my eyes upon: a Phillips-head screwdriver. Yes. This would work nicely. It even had a handle.

I zipped out the back door and threw myself into the van. Dav was turning the ignition over and over: *chu chu-huh, chu chu-huh.* Nothing.

DAV: Did you get it?

ME: *Of course I got it. Like I would go inside to get it and then not get it.*

DAV: I don't see it.

ME: *I got a screwdriver.*

DAV: Then you didn't get it, stupid-head! I said a pencil and that's not a pencil.

ME: *It's sort of a pencil.*

DAV: It's not sort of a pencil. It's not even sort of a screwdriver. It is exactly a screwdriver. Stick it there and I'll turn the ignition.

ME: *Where?*

DAV: There. There! Where we always stick the pencil.

ME: *It's not a pencil. It's not even sort of a pencil.*

DAV: Stick it!

So I stuck it. Shoved it, actually. I was a little bit perturbed at my own inability to find something as simple as a pencil.

I did not realize how deep down into the carburetor I had shoved the screwdriver. Dav turned the ignition and the engine started up immediately. It revved loudly.

And louder.

And louder.

The usual dip that occurs when a car engine revs up—it was nowhere to be heard. The car just kept revving higher and louder, higher and louder, eventually shrieking like a banshee.

DAV: That's enough. Take the screwdriver out now.

ME: *Take it out?*

DAV: Take it OUT.

ME: *I put it in too far. I can't take it out.*

DAV: WHAT DO YOU MEAN you put it in TOO
          FAR?! You're just supposed to use it to hold it
          open! How FAR did you put it?!

ME: *Nobody said HOLD IT OPEN! I put it IN! All the
          way IN!*

DAV: ALL THE WAY IN?! ALL?! THE?! WAY?! It's a
          CARBURETOR—not a JUICER!

ME: *I'm SORRY! I've never stuck a screwdriver in
          ANYTHING!*

DAV: That's because you DON'T STICK A
          SCREWDRIVER IN ANYTHING!!

ME: *How am I supposed to know that?! Was there some
          tool safety RETREAT?!*

DAV: Don't get SNIPPY! Just get the SCREWDRIVER
          OUT!!

ME: *I CAN'T!!! GET!!! IT!!! OUT!!!*

We were now screaming at the top of our lungs because the engine sounded like the tornado-warning sirens on the local water tower. Dav and I stared at the rpm's. We listened to the impassioned, bloodcurdling scream of the engine. We had seen enough *CHiPs* episodes to know what was likely going to happen next. We yelled the same words at the exact same time.

BOTH: *SHE'S GOING TO BLOOOOOOW!!*

And then—we escaped.

We bolted out of that van—leaving the doors wide open, the van engine shrieking. We practically dove through the garage, slamming the kitchen door behind us. We expected at any moment to hear the sound of a triple explosion: *BA BOOM BLOODGE!* I don't actually know how it would even be possible for an automobile to explode three entire times, but it happened every week in front of Erik Estrada.

HVRAAAAAAAAAAAAAAAANG!!!!!

The van would not shut up. All of our neighbors were now watching with hands firmly clenched over their ears. There it was, sitting in our driveway. The eyesore was now an earsore. The van was dying a loud, obnoxious death—alienating anyone who had ever loved it—all the while advertising on the side in big cursive letters: *Christian Center Academy*.

Dav and I stood, huddled together in the kitchen, waiting for the van to detonate into whatever pieces of it still remained after our last trip down the highway. We waited and waited.

But the van did not blow up.

Suddenly Dad walked in. *What is that racket?!* We explained the carburetor trick. We defended the lack of pencils. We confessed to the screwdriver shoving. We warned the van was about to implode. And Dad simply stared at us.

DAD: You can't get the screwdriver out?

US: *NO!*

DAD: Why don't you just turn off the ignition?

Oh.

Well, that would be a slightly simpler solution.

We tiptoed wearily back to the van and turned the key. The engine cooled down until the van suddenly *chugga-chugga-chugged.*

And then—*BAAAANG!*

The van backfired so loudly, we thought we had each been shot in the chest. In a way that would have been better, because we would not have had to return to the kitchen where Dad was waiting.

Needless to say, we never stuck anything in that carburetor again. Ironically we didn't have to. Whether it was the lengthy high revving or the massive backfire, something cleaned out that system. From that moment on, the van engine purred like a kitten.

MINISTRY IS SURGERY

If only we could have had a moment that shocking to clean out what had been going on *inside* the van for so long. Perhaps then we would have been more considerate to the definition our actions were giving to the words written on its exterior. When the van was first painted, the thought had been that the words *Christian Center*

Academy would be a witness, a tool to lead people to the church and school and therefore to Jesus. But the one important thing that had never been considered was that the words on the side of the van would be inextricably linked to the goings-on inside of it. The words would be redefined by the actions they seemingly endorsed. Due to the fact that we did not consider our antics in this fashion— i.e., we did not realize what our bad behavior was *saying*—we never took the time to correct those actions.

It's sad. Our activities were intended to belong only to ourselves—just a way of being a teenager. But because of the label being advertised, our deeds held a heftier weight. To assume that the behavior inside the vehicle would automatically be Christian would certainly disappoint the observer. Like biting into an Oreo to discover someone had removed the cream filling. Just another way we had waved the sharp edges of our faith in a manner that wounded more than it healed.

This is how I came to the conclusion that ministry is surgery.

You may or may not believe this applies to you because you may not consider yourself a minister and you may want your life to have nothing to do with ministry. Unfortunately that is irrelevant. From the moment that you make a stand for Christ—call yourself a Christian, communicate that you are going to follow Him, whatever that may look like—from that moment on, your life is being observed. And if your life is being observed as a sample of Jesus, then your life is undoubtedly ministry.

Whether you want it to be or not.

And ministry is surgery. It is supposed to be careful, precise, meticulous, detailed, insightful, tender, intentional, and sensitive. Ministry is the procedure of helping others uncover the cancer in their lives—and then carefully loving that cancer out of them. This is why our faith has sharp edges. It is required to be a scalpel.

But just like the removal of the dog's tongue, we have been waving our scalpels around irresponsibly, like it's a pencil with an eraser—as if any damage done is simply an accident and can be undone just as easily. We believe that if we carelessly screw up, we can say a quick prayer and apology, and the mistake will be chalked up to our humanness. It never dawns on us that the mistake might redefine Christianity to someone who is observing.

It might just incorrectly redefine Jesus.

It is for this very reason that we (as a church community) are mostly talk and very little fruit. We say whatever we feel impassioned about, but we only do what we feel like doing at any given moment. We are not meticulous and careful in our faith because we have become the religion of the do-over.

We love that Jesus died for our sins and that His grace cancels out the Old Testament need for a sacrifice. Those Old Testamenters—WOW—they really had to bend over backward to get right with God: sackcloth and ashes, burnt offerings, weeping and gnashing. I couldn't gnash even if I wanted to. If I did, my orthodontist would make me wear a retainer to bed. We thank God that Jesus made all of those spiritual gymnastics a moot point. Jesus died on the cross. He took the blame. His scars and blood and death replaced the need for mine. That's what grace is—and we love, love, love grace.

Sadly, we also abuse it.

In an attempt to be a more free church—less bound up in legal-
ism—we have embraced grace so heartily that we have also eradicated
responsibility. We cave to sin and temptation and desires and whims
and preferences very easily, especially in the church, and we feel bad
fleetingly. Then grace comes in and spanks guilt and we have a half
hour of worship and feel awesome. But we don't do a whole lot of
the dirty work to truly seek permanent healing—to truly sprint away
from sin with all of our might.

Grace is the greatest gift anyone could have ever given us. It
should humble us, prompt us to make our lives right. It should make
us want to please that sort of caring Savior so much that every time
we fail and need grace, it drives us toward purity—toward accountability. Grace should be met by gratefulness, and gratefulness should
prompt responsible action.

Instead, daily sins, shortcomings, and afflictions are rampantly
increasing in the modern church. Why? Because we are seeing grace
as a coupon—as a voucher that allows us to not worry about destruc-
tive actions leading to disastrous consequences. It is as if we believe
that for everyone else sin leads to hell and death, but for us it leads
to a scolding that is quickly forgotten. We act like sinful actions are
a cakewalk because we are lucky enough to know about the grace
discount.

To live in such a way disrespects grace. It shames grace—it
insinuates that Jesus suffered and died so that we could sin more
freely. And it communicates a world of lies to the observers that hear
the roaring and then notice the writing on the side of the van. What
happened to the reverence? The heartbreak that is supposed to come
from displeasing God? Have we gone so far to the other extreme that

the only part of sin that matters to us is whether or not it is going to keep us out of heaven? The truth is, Christ's grace does cover us, but our sins speak lies upon lies to those who have not yet decided if Christ is worth following. To them our choice of what to do about grace may very well mean life or death.

Our lives are observed.

A life observed is ministry.

Ministry is surgery.

When the Christian*ish* respond to grace by going ahead and sinning and expecting fewer repercussions, we slice and dice everything within arm's reach. Why? Do we intend to harm? No. I do not believe that we do. Do we not care about others? I do not believe this is true, either. We react carelessly because we believe two of the Enemy's biggest lies about our own lives:

1.   Our actions don't matter.
2.   Our lives aren't ministry.

But nothing could be further from the truth. Your life is observed, therefore your life is ministry. And because ministry is surgery, your actions matter very much. Because your actions matter very much, your faith cannot stop at grace. Grace does not replace change. Grace enables change. It empowers it, makes the change worth it. Grace transforms change from a penalty to an act of gratitude. And that is what is tremendously missing from modern Christianity:

Tangible gratitude for God's grace.

We must refuse to waste grace as a coupon to remain stuck in our sinful cycles. We should instead invite Christ to use His grace as a microscope so that we can seek true healing from our obvious sins, and then daily dig deeper into the more subtle core issues that continue to kill us. We must thank God daily, not merely in our prayers, but in our eradication of the things we may like, but He hates. Jesus put it this way:

> *If you don't go all the way with me, through thick and thin, you don't deserve me. If your first concern is to look after yourself, you'll never find yourself. But if you forget about yourself and look to me, you'll find both yourself and me.*
>
> Matthew 10:38–39 MSG

We don't seem to have a problem going all the way with Jesus in times of thin. If we are lost or hungry or poor or emotionally crumbling, we are suddenly all His. We surrender our sinful ways and we get right with God. This is the pre-Christian approach. Then we meet up with grace and we realize that we no longer need to live in shame. We realize that we cannot earn our salvation and, better yet, Jesus has already bought it for us.

That's when we get thick.

It's a lot more difficult to go all the way with Jesus in times of thick. Even covered in God's grace, our first concern can never be to look only after ourselves. It is that sort of thinking that treats grace wastefully. We have to accept the reality that our actions shout loudly—that there are people staring, not only reading what is written on the side of the van, but observing carefully what is going on inside when it's rocking down the highway.

Of course, if that becomes our modus operandi—that we are only following Jesus carefully because we're afraid of what others will think—then we're suddenly back to shame, and grace loses its power. We must instead respect *grace*, choose to truly think through what it means for our lives, and then respond.

It is the same as when Jesus performed miracles: turning water into wine, healing sickness and disease, walking on water, raising the dead, casting out demonic powers. Jesus did all of these actions because of one significant reason: love. He wasn't looking for an exchange of actions. He did not give the miracle in order to receive loyalty. Jesus did the miraculous time and time again with no ulterior motive. And yet time and time again, something was indeed reciprocated:

> *He touched her hand and the fever left her, and she got up and began to wait on him.*
>
> Matthew 8:15

> *So the man went away and began to tell in the Decapolis how much Jesus had done for him. And all the people were amazed.*
>
> Mark 5:20

> *But they went out and spread the news about him all over that region.*
>
> Matthew 9:31

Jesus had compassion on them and touched their eyes.
Immediately they received their sight and followed
him.

Matthew 20:34

There is no miracle in history greater than God's grace as proven through Jesus on the cross. And yet much smaller miracles were consistently followed by an act of reciprocation. In other words, when the people were confronted head-on with God's grace, they *chose to acknowledge the love.* They were so moved by what Jesus did that they wanted to do something back. They did not sidestep it or diminish it by neglecting to appreciate what an astronomical gift they had just been given.

How much more do we as the modern church need to daily acknowledge the love of God with tangible gratitude for His grace? But we cannot reciprocate if we do not comprehend the value of Christ's life traded for ours, and we cannot comprehend this trade if we do not acknowledge the value of our own life—that it is indeed ministry.

Through Christ's grace are we saved.

Once saved, we are observed.

An observed life is ministry.

And ministry is surgery.

The natural act of tangible gratitude to God's grace is *to love Him back*—to receive His love in the form of forgiveness of our sins—but to choose diligence in overcoming those sins as a loving statement of gratefulness. The days of resting sloppily on our salvation must end. Works certainly don't buy us a place in heaven, but grace without those works is dead. We've attempted faith our own way—by wasting grace. It's time to respect grace and live God's way. And that is when the goings-on inside the van begin to match the words printed on the outside.

> *But what happens when we live God's way? He brings gifts into our lives, much the same way that fruit appears in an orchard—things like affection for others, exuberance about life, serenity. We develop a willingness to stick with things, a sense of compassion in the heart, and a conviction that a basic holiness permeates things and people. We find ourselves involved in loyal commitments, not needing to force our way in life, able to marshal and direct our energies wisely.*
>
> Galatians 5:22–23 MSG

That sounds more like following Jesus. A life filled with selfless and sinless actions—not because the life is driven by shame, but rather because the life is overjoyed and grateful for the benefits of grace. That is a healthy life, a life worth observing. A life that is truly ministry. A life that is empowered to carefully locate the cancer of sin in those around it—in order to gently love that cancer out.

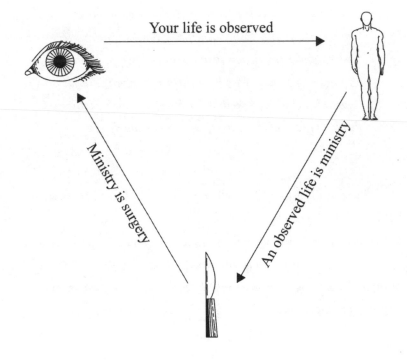

1. What does it mean to say that ministry is surgery? What does it mean to say that faith has sharp edges?

2. How have you used the sharp edges of your faith? Are there times they have carelessly wounded? Are there times they have surgically healed?

3. If ministry is the procedure of helping others uncover the cancer in their lives—and then carefully loving that cancer out of them, what does that require of the minister?

4. Consider these adjectives for ministry: careful, precise, meticulous, detailed, insightful, tender, intentional, and sensitive. Do these words define ministry you have personally experienced?

5. Can you relate to the thought that Christianity has become the religion of the "do-over"? Do you feel that we have abused Jesus' grace?

6. Discuss the following rumination on grace: "Grace should humble us, prompt us to make our lives right. It should make us want to please that sort of caring Savior so much that every time we fail and need grace, it drives us toward purity—toward accountability. Grace should be met by gratefulness and gratefulness should prompt responsible action."

7. What happened to reverence and remorse? The heartbreak that is supposed to come from displeasing God? Have we gone so far the other extreme

that the only part of sin that matters to us is whether
or not it is going to keep us out of heaven?

8.   Do you believe that your actions don't matter?
Do you believe that your life is not ministry?

9.   *"Grace does not replace change. Grace enables
change. It empowers it, makes the change worth it.
Grace transforms change from a penalty to an act of
gratitude."* How can you show tangible gratitude for
God's grace?

the Jesus show 10

I knew I was going to be a performer the first time I realized that in order to get a treat, you had to do a trick. If our parakeet wanted out of the cage, he had to do a flip. If the dog wanted a biscuit, he had to sit and stay. If Brad wanted a car, he had to get good grades, and if I wanted to see *Return of the Jedi* on opening day, I had to mow three lawns and memorize Lamentations. This was the circle of reward: Be impressive in order to be indulged.

Like every other performer in the world, my drug of choice was applause and I quickly broached every method possible in order to get my fix. People used to tell me that I cared too much about what people thought of me. They misunderstood. What I actually cared about was what thinking of me made people *do*: ovations, accolades, fruit baskets, sainthood—I wasn't finicky. Many times I would have settled for a smile and a gold star.

I loved Jesus with my whole heart—well, the whole heart except for the parts that were infatuated with myself. I liked me. Really liked me. An unhealthy love. Many would call this pride, but I would call it peer pressure because everyone loved me and I was just trying to fit in.

This was the dichotomy. I loved Jesus. And I loved me. And I loved performing. And I loved applause. Okay, so maybe more of a quadchotomy. In a perfect world I would have always performed in a manner that glorified Jesus. This would have been followed by the applause of men and angels, and every ovation for me would have led the world to the salvation power of the Christ because they adored me and wanted to personally co-opt whatever made me so special. However, this is not the way the world actually works. In many instances, if I indeed wanted the applause, I had to sidestep the part that might have glorified Jesus. You can't cheer two heroes any more than you can serve two masters, and it didn't take long before I realized that I wasn't going to get a curtain call until I kicked Jesus backstage.

Certainly I continued to serve Jesus with my life—and even pursued theatrical approaches that would spread His message. But internally the pursuit was far more about my own personal need for praise.

When I first told my parents that I thought I wanted to be an actor and a writer when I grew up, their response was that I could do anything I wanted as long as I gave all the glory to God. I obliged because, at the time, the request felt like a tag-on, something you tacked to the end of the résumé. *Additional skills: horseback riding, juggling, jujitsu, giving God the glory.* It was something I accessed if it matched the creative endeavor in question. I had not thoroughly processed how this was supposed to play out.

My first test came when I was the crisp age of ten. Our house butted up against a football field that extended from a community recreation center. My brother Dav and I spent an inordinate amount of time inside this recreation center, shooting pool and watching Margo (who ran the place under the employ of the city) beat an out-of-work dude named John John at cribbage. John John was the local pool shark. At the time, he seemed thirty, but judging by the fact that he could never grow a proper mustache, he was more than likely closer to seventeen. John John never seemed to leave the building. If the rec center was open, he was there chain-smoking and mocking all the preteens who scratched on the first shot of nine-ball. I used to believe this was due to some secret loyalty he had to Margo, but now I think he was just dodging juvie. John John would offer us one of his cigarettes, usually the one he was almost finished smoking. We would consistently refuse. One time, when I declined, he put his cigarette out on the back of my hand and called me the Mother term that is not followed by Teresa.

Good times.

Margo would then scold John John, telling him to watch his mouth and then confirm to us that smoking was indeed bad for us while she took a drag from her Camel Light through the open breathing hole in her neck.

The rec center was not the sort of wonderland I would have normally frequented. The clientele were eclectic, unified only in their corporate scariness to ten-year-olds. Certainly we only went there because it was in the backyard and summers got pretty boring by June 18.

One day Dav, our buddy/bully (depending upon his dose of meds) Matt Rebidue, and I were so bored, we decided to put on a show for the rec center.

ME:	*We should totally put on a show. That would be cool.*
DAV:	I don't think cool is what that would be.
ME:	*But we could show John John that we're not losers like he says. We can sing and act and tell jokes and dance.*
DAV:	That'll show him.
ME:	*I bet he likes rock 'n' roll. I'll go get Brad's Imperials album.*
DAV:	I don't know if singing and dancing will make John John think we are cool.
ME:	*Why not?*
DAV:	Have you ever seen what people look like when they dance?
ME:	*Yes. Every day in the bathroom mirror.*
DAV:	It's different when it's not yourself.
ME:	*You don't think we should sing and dance?*
DAV:	I think we'll feel stupid just standing there.
ME:	*You're absolutely right … We'd better make it puppets.*

This was how the decision was made to construct a stage out of an old Yoda bedsheet and create three creatures out of used tube socks, yarn, and plastic Easter eggs. We suddenly considered it genius to pin ourselves into one of the concrete corners of the inside of the rec center, armed only with sock puppets lip-synching to "Trumpet of Jesus." We even planned an intermission right smack in the middle of the eight songs so that John John could calm himself with a Pabst Blue Ribbon.

We were ready and raring to go. We had received permission from Margo, and the stage was constructed. I ran home to scour my

room for props that would invoke the most laughter, when Mom
asked what we were about to do.

ME: *OH! It's awesome! We're gonna put on a puppet
           show!*

MOM: A puppet show? Really?

ME: *Yup.*

MOM: At the recreation center?

ME: *Yuh-huh.*

MOM: Will there be a lot of kids there?

ME: *TONS. Practically eleven.*

MOM: You should ask if they want to hear a Bible story.

"Of course," I said out loud. Meanwhile, inside I barfed. Had
my mother gone mad? Did she not understand what sort of delin-
quents and hooligans and riffraff attended complimentary puppet
shows at the rec center? I adored my mom and could not imagine
declining this request, partly because I knew it would break her
heart but mostly because I thought if I did decline, the refrigerator
would immediately swallow me whole and I would slide down the
oversized veggie crisper into the third circle of hell.

I made no mention of this to Dav or Matt Rebidue. I simply
sat somber, stressed, and preoccupied through the entirety of the
performance with my arm outstretched, my sock puppet *(Floopie
the Fozeneeper)* slightly less expressive than in rehearsal. Matt and
Dav struggled to understand why I was having trouble establishing
witty repartee or over-the-top physical comedy with the Hanes on
my left hand. Dav finally asked me what was on my mind.

ME: *We're supposed to ask if they want to hear a Bible*
            story.

DAV: What do you mean we're supposed to ask?!

ME: *We're supposed to. Mom said.*

DAV: Nooooo. You did not tell her we would.

ME: *Of course not. But I might have. Yes.*

DAV: John John will murder us with a pool cue. He'll
            burn our puppet hand.

ME: *Do you think they would rush the stage like at that*
            Who concert where the girl got trampled to death?

DAV: Probably.

ME: *Ask them.*

DAV: Ask them what?!

ME: *If they want to hear a Bible story.*

DAV: Have you been drinking Margo's Pabst?! NO
            WAY!

ME: *But I don't want to go to hell and you're older.*

DAV: I won't go to hell! I repented while you were
            talking about the Who concert.

ME: *I think I'm having a heart attack.*

So I dipped my voice down into a mooselike Heffalump tone as
Floopie oompahed the seemingly innocuous question: *Would any-*
body out there like to hear a Bible story? To which every last person in
the audience spit out: NO! I retorted (still the Heffalump): *No big*
deal. I promised my mom I would ask.

DAV: What the heck did you say THAT for?!

ME:	*It just came out! Are they gonna think we're stupid?*
DAV:	They're gonna think YOU'RE stupid!
ME:	*Maybe they'll think it's just part of the show.*
DAV:	What—like it was the puppet's mom who made him ask? Puppets don't HAVE moms. Puppets come from wool, which comes from SHEEP!
ME:	*So I should've said that I promised my sheep I would ask.*
DAV:	Yeah, they might have bought that.

I was ashamed for days. Ashamed that I promised Mom though I didn't really want to do it. Ashamed that I didn't want to do it. Ashamed that I was ashamed. Ashamed that my puppet had a hole in it. Generally lots of random shame. I decided then and there that I would only bring Jesus into my performance if it really worked, but that I would try my best to make it really work much more often.

ONSTAGE & BACKSTAGE

This began a dozen-year process of writing and performing what I had written, trying my best to discover a formula that would indeed theologically exalt God while artistically celebrating myself.

The path culminated in college, where I pursued a telecommunications major that spread itself evenly between film, television, and theater, all under the covering of a program that was searching for the best way to communicate Jesus through all three. I gravitated most toward the theater program, primarily because gratification was instantaneous. I was given a great deal of leeway to thrive on the stage, and I found a warm, cozy home for my ego, continuing to struggle with giving the glory upward while so many eyes seemed locked on me.

During this season, I performed in bitter tragedies, ribald comedies, and the occasional musical, venturing into Molière, Shakespeare, Arthur Miller, Tennessee Williams—but the real opportunity to praise Jesus through my art arrived my senior year with the production of Stephen Schwartz's musical *Godspell*. A modernized retelling of the gospel of Christ through improvisation, dance, and song, *Godspell* has been a longtime crowd-pleaser, bringing the life of Jesus to fresh eyes and ears. Finally we would be utilizing the gifts God gave us for an artistic piece that pointed directly to Him. As a bonus I had the privilege of working with one of the most talented casts in my personal history. The cast was classically trained. The cast was skilled at improvisation. The cast was dynamic.

The cast was a royal pain in the derriere.

Not all the cast, mind you. Dav was there with me, just as he was throughout most of my favorite artistic moments. A few others in the cast were great friends with quality attitudes. But I've never seen so many catfights, so much belligerence and dissension in such a small gathering of artistic people. Ten cast members and at least five prima donnas. Onstage they called them Pharisees. Backstage, they called them divas.

The irony, of course, was that this was the single greatest opportunity to literally utilize our art to exemplify Christ. And yet here we were, rehearsing in a boiling pot of resentment, sniping, and backstabbing. I yearned for the moments I was actually running a scene, because whenever I was on the sidelines, someone would give me an

earful about the director or someone else in the cast. You could feel
the umbrage rising. Creative people are a pill anyway. Give us an
ounce of offense and we'll carry it on our back like *Pilgrim's Progress.*
But get a whole room of offended artists together and HOO BOY!
Talk about giving what you are *feeling* too much credit. The fury of a
woman scorned has nothing on a prima donna who doesn't appreciate the director's notes.

This tension reached its climax the afternoon I was aiding
another stagehand in removing the platforms that were covering
the orchestra pit. The backstabbing had reached a fever pitch and
my brother was not around to cool my jets (Dav has always been my
fire extinguisher, which is odd because I am his nitroglycerin). The
stagehand was giving me an earful because, as you could imagine,
when a cast fights internally, it makes more work for the crew. I was
impatient with him and I suggested we hurry up and remove the final
piece of staging. He urged me to wait for more of the crew to arrive,
but as this would require our awkward conversation to continue, I
prodded him forward. We both reached down to pick up the final
platform. I lifted with my back, thinking this piece of staging would
be the same lightweight as the other four had been. I felt something
in my back pull apart. A fiery hot sensation shot up my spine like
static electricity.

FRAAAAAAAAAAAAANG!

Something was desperately wrong. It turned out that center
platform was the one stabilizing the other four. It was a sort of cor-
nerstone, which is bizarre because it was in the middle. To this end,
as the support protecting the orchestra from tumbling performers, it
was dense and filled with concrete.

The next morning, when I awoke, my walk had a subtle differ-ence. My spine felt like it had a new curvature leaning left. My neck was locked in a leaning tilt. Performance week was a few days away and I was in great pain.

I attempted to stretch it out, swallowing my grief throughout rehearsal because I did not want the cast or the director to think that I was weak. We didn't have understudies at our university, but with the muckraking going on in our cast, I was certain that if I showed a sign of weakness, another actor would find a way to insert himself.

I gritted my teeth through all of the performances. The sad reality is that this was the sort of show of which I had always dreamed. Fun, comedic, artistic, and best of all, promoting Jesus. It should have been a week of celebration. Instead, due to all the poison and cancer in the proceedings, I stood there in pain, forcing the words out of my mouth and praying secretly that the week would end quickly.

It did not.

After an excruciating weekend the show finished its run. Joy had not come. And agony had lingered.

The pain slowly subsided in the following months until March, when I awoke one day with seizing muscles. I was unable to move my neck, and one leg appeared several inches shorter than the other.

It turned out that when I had lifted that one piece of staging, my vertebrae had separated. As they pulled apart, one of the nerves that flows up and down my back and on down my leg—that nerve slipped in between the separated vertebrae. When I set the staging down, the vertebrae closed, pinching that nerve. Over the several months that followed, the nerve worked its way farther in while the disks began to merge. Over time it worsened. The next thing I knew, I woke up on a spring day to discover that the damage could not be easily repaired—and had thrust me into significant misery.

I immediately went to the chiropractor to discover that the process out of pain would be significant, precarious, and time-consuming. I would be required to go to therapy three times a week for an undisclosed period of time.

It ended up taking two months.

I was in extreme pain for two months, teetering back and forth with one leg shorter than the other, my neck often pinched and unable to turn well. The agony was consistent and intolerable, and it made it very difficult to walk, bend, or sleep.

All because I had been artistically perturbed in a season when my performance could have actually mattered for eternity.

I continued to eke out a feeble existence amid this pain, resisting any major physical exertion until finally the pain became tolerable. I found that if I stopped using the areas of my body that were torturing me, the agony would subside. I had embraced a new normal. Less pain as long as I chose to utilize less of my body.

But life wasn't going to let up just yet. The next thing I knew, the beginning of May had arrived, and I could pretend no more. It was time for missions training week.

THE STRETCHING

I had signed up for summer missions almost a year prior, having no idea I would be suffering such bodily grief when the time arrived to leave the country. Yet here I was suddenly at a boot camp in the woods, a harness around my nethers, leaping from trees and under-going significant and exhaustive drama training.

The first morning of drama training, I knew I was in trouble. Due to my theater background my team was looking to me to be the example. I observed as our trainer walked in the door: a spunky, high-energy dancerciser named Andrea. She had the appearance of someone who had just last week earned a gold medal in balance beam before speed-walking to this very training camp, pit-stopping only to choreograph Cirque du Soleil for a high-impact afternoon. Her first stretching exercise (cited as the warm-up) was to lie prone on the floor while her legs split, each foot touching one of the Dakotas.

I broke into a cold sweat. Impossible. I watched as her limbs and torso contorted, making shapes that a strand of yarn couldn't feasibly accomplish. I wouldn't have been surprised to discover that, in some freakish dancer surgery, Andrea had her skeleton removed entirely and replaced with cartilage and Tupperware.

Then suddenly she was up again. Risen to a standing position without actually moving any joints. It was as if her body had poured itself into a new stance. She was liquid metal.

"Now," Andrea stated, "it's your turn." Our turn to fold our-selves into the shape of an amoeba with scoliosis. This was supposed to eventually lead someone to Jesus. I attempted a first move only to feel daggers shoot up my spine. As I allowed my body to become an acute angle, I began to elongate muscles I had intentionally left to rot. It was like fire. No. Worse than that. It was like I was a fire sandwich being chewed by a molten lava hyena whose teeth were made of wasp stingers and rusty dentist drills (i.e., unpleasant). I went into a massive spasm.

Andrea, seeing my twinge, asked if I was in fact elderly. When I assured her I was merely twenty-one, she aided me in my approach to stretching by urging my limbs farther than I had been willing to urge them myself. Those tendons I had tried so hard to let die were now screaming profanities at my endorphins.

What is the opposite of euphoria? Agony? Torture? Rigor mortis? Somehow none of those words seemed thorough enough to describe how I felt at that precise moment. I made my spine and muscles do things that they had not been required to do for eight months—and they were livid.

It became clear to me that I was not going to make it through this week without great pain, and without making it through this week, I was not going to be equipped to adequately minister drama on the mission field. I had assumed the theater portion of this week was going to be cake because that was my history of expertise. Little did I know that, even in my place of strength, I would be significantly stretched.

As the week progressed, I began to pray more fervently for healing in my spine. At the start of the week this was due to the intense pain— but as the seven days passed, something peculiar started to happen. Through Andrea's words and the other teaching we received, I began to realign my creative thinking toward the direction of what Christ could do through me if I was truly submitted to Him. Through Andrea's physical stretching techniques, what began as agony slowly became freedom. I began to find joy (even through the pain) exploring the manner in which the areas God had given me skill could actually make a substantial and direct difference to others in the name of Jesus. For the first time the art lost its place at the forefront and instead surrendered the pole position to Jesus. Probably because pain was required as a path to purpose. I began to find new pleasure in creativity for the right reasons. I discovered harmony with a theatrical team for the first time in ages. And as my mind was renewed, as I began praying for the right things, as my heart and body were stretched … the pain in my back began to disappear.

As I woke up in the mornings nearing the end of the camp, my neck was not stiffened, my legs were inexplicably the same length. I was sleeping comfortably. And I suddenly rediscovered the ability and desire to bend.

During the six weeks of that mission trip, I fell in love with ministry again—and in the process saw my artistic obsessions transform into healthy perspective. Even afterward I continued to dramatize for a living—but I discovered a path far more life-giving than performance, than simply doing the trick for the treat. I began a lifetime of sleuthing out the ways art could reveal the truth of the love of Christ. I stopped yearning to prod whatever applause I could get out of an audience and instead I saw the audience as the recipients of what I could give. In the process I finally discovered what I had been created to become in the first place.

All because I had been stretched.

What was true of my body had been true of my faith—and what had been true of my faith continues to be true behind the scenes of the church at large. Follow the chain of events:

- God grants me a love of performing as well as giving me the ability to perform as a means of spreading His truth and love.

- I discover that I like what performing does for me more than I like what it does for Him.
- This changes both the reason for and the manner in which I perform.
- Due to the fact that I am no longer performing for the reasons I was created to perform, it quickly loses its power as a life-giver to me.
- I cease performing for His sake, but keep performing for my own sake—therefore feeding my insecurities while I believe I am calming them.
- This manner of performing leads to lack of personal fulfillment, an absence of perspective, and sudden strife.
- The strife leads to personal chaos, which leads to pain.
- In order to deal with the pain, I choose functionality instead of true healing.
- Functionality causes me to ignore the real problem, so atrophy sets in.
- Atrophy is the new normal. The irony is that in this state I can no longer perform at all. I cannot find happiness.
- To transform, it will require radical stretching—which means great pain.
- All this, just to get back to the place where I am performing for the right reasons.

This is exactly where the poison and bile the unchurched world senses within Christianity comes from. We have become a body of individuals who say we are living with true authenticity, and then we are quick to turn it into nothing more than an apathetic show that hides the pain of our dysfunction. We follow and serve a Savior who entered the world as a woodworker, lived His life as a transient, and died a criminal—but we keep trying to shove His simplicity into our adulation-hungry extravaganza. All the while we mistakenly believe that if we can make the onstage seem like enough of a spectacle, no one will notice the garbage going on behind the scenes.

It's time to stop faking the Jesus show.

LOVE IS A MUSCLE

We've been treating the Jesus message as if it is for our own adoration—supposed to bring us applause. It's not. In fact it is more than likely going to bring us the sort of pain that stems from significant stretching. We resist this stretching because we do not like agony. But pain must come where there is atrophy. If it does not, then the unused muscle dies. The unused muscle of the modern church is selfless, attentive, transforming love. It dies because we keep our distance from the unlovely—and we keep our distance because getting too close to them is painful.

But the church is supposed to be about love, so we continue to *say* we are loving—we continue to *perform* love, but it is a counterfeit. As long as we continue to resist the pain of authentic risky relationships, church is only a puppet show—the Word of God coming out of some foreign variation of our voice while the real self stoops anonymously behind a bedsheet.

This is the gravest danger in saying we are following Jesus when in fact we are following applause. We hop onstage and say we are about Jesus, but our methods and even message change rapidly if the audience does not readily accept us. If we quote Jesus and then discover His ideology is unpopular, we attempt to popularize it with cleverness. We soften its sharp edges, rendering it about as capable of surgery as a butter knife. In the process we garner a great many fans, but we don't truly love them because we won't dare risk speaking the whole truth.

The reality of who Jesus is—why He came to this earth, what He did while He was here, what He said while He was here, and exactly who happens to be His Father—this is all unchanging in a world that sees details of the gospel fall in and out of fad and fashion depending upon what works best for modern society. When we pick and choose the details, ensuring that we are always speaking to no more than the choir in order to not offend— and certainly not jade any fans—we do the sacrifice of Christ a disservice.

There is only one reason we attempt to soften the details of Jesus: because the truth of who He is might not be popular with those in the audience of the moment. This is a ministry approach that is 100 percent about the messenger (i.e., us) and completely disrespectful to the Message Himself. We have turned our addiction to performing and our need for ovation into little white lies: turning the verse "speaking the truth in love" into "speaking just enough truth to get myself some love." In the process we are omitting the transformative particulars. The truth is we only truly love the people in this world when we simultaneously risk unpopularity. This is what it means to be in this world, but not of it. We must risk connection with people, but for God's glory instead of our own. We do not tend to do this. Instead we insert our own well-being ahead of the truth. The result: people in the church doing the correct *what* for the incorrect *why*. This can only lead to one thing, and it is the worst witness the church can have to a disbelieving world: behind-the-scenes bedlam.

Sniping and bitterness and infighting on catastrophic levels. Churches bickering throughout their internal structures while the congregations barely ghost through the doors weekly to pretend they are known. Ministries and Christian businesses throwing layer upon layer of public disguises atop bad business practices and even worse treatment of employees. Chaos pervading the families of ministers. Communities of believers seizing upon the slightest weakness to quickly demean and alienate one another through the rumor mill. A cacophony of turmoil just behind the curtain wherever the Christian life is being sold to an eager audience as easy and flexible.

Why must we continually skew one extreme or the other? Why is it that half the Christians seem to be holier-than-thous who appear to hate those who don't follow Jesus while the other half wants so desperately to be accepted by the world that they water down the truth and therefore do not truly minister? Why can't we love the people while we simultaneously tell the whole truth? The truth to someone who doesn't follow Jesus is straightforward: *Jesus hates sin but He loves you. He wants me to love you too—and I will, but I won't love the sin that is destroying you, even if you don't believe that it is.* We have to draw a line, *loveline* though it is. Again, ministry is surgery, but regardless of how delicate the removal of the cancer, it's still going to hurt to have it taken out.

THE WRECKAGE IN BETWEEN

If anyone could have taken the performance approach to ministry, it was Jesus. After all, adoration of Him was simultaneously adoration of God. He was permitted to shine. But Jesus took no action for the benefit of His own reputation. He took action for the benefit of the truth.

- He healed because the people were sick.
- He told stories because the multitudes would not otherwise understand.
- He rebuked the Pharisees because their pride was killing them.

His extreme ways fostered both friends and enemies, applause and death threats. He never stopped loving and He never stopped speaking truth. Some loved Him and some hated Him, but all received the message they most needed in His presence.

Even down to the point of death, Jesus was repeatedly given the opportunity to say the magic words and make it all go away. But Jesus never worked the crowd for the response that felt best. Instead He took even the most brutal personal moments and chose to continue loving.

> *Two other men, both criminals, were also led out with him to be executed. When they came to the place called the Skull, there they crucified him, along with the criminals—one on his right, the other on his left.*
>
> Luke 23:32–33

> *One of the criminals who hung there hurled insults at*
> *him: "Aren't you the Christ? Save yourself and us!" But*
> *the other criminal rebuked him. "Don't you fear God,"*
> *he said, "since you are under the same sentence? We*
> *are punished justly, for we are getting what our deeds*
> *deserve. But this man has done nothing wrong." Then*
> *he said, "Jesus, remember me when you come into your*
> *kingdom." Jesus answered him, "I tell you the truth,*
> *today you will be with me in paradise."*
>
> Luke 23:39–43

All the way to the bitter end—to the moment when He Himself felt forsaken—Jesus did not defend Himself. He did not justify or clarify who He was or the reasons He should be brought down off that cross. Though criticism and scorn were thrown His direction, though He was bullied and made to look the weak fool, He continued to forge through what He knew to be extremely necessary evils. He laid His reputation down and allowed it to be brutally savaged. And even at the point of utmost pain and humiliation—the hours on the cross—even as He was belittled by a common thief to His side, Jesus showed mercy and love and forgiveness and made even this terrible moment about someone else's salvation. That is because Jesus never reached out to the person who could do the most for His reputation. He never performed for the greatest applause. Instead He reached out to whoever happened to be right next to Him. Even at the point of death. Because Jesus was not a performer. The accolades did not matter to Him. The life transformed by love mattered to Him. Regardless of what it might look like to whomever was watching.

Jesus was not a performer because Jesus realized that the whole world *is* an audience, but the goal is not their applause. The goal is to eventually bring them all onstage to share in the experience, to love them into being a part of the transformation process. To eventually have so many sharing the stage that the spotlight cannot focus on a single one. All egos become lost in the family.

But this camaraderie cannot be accomplished onstage just yet. There are profound truths waiting to be related to the world at large, but we aren't ready to deliver the message. We must first get the backstage cleaned out. If we don't, we will speak the truth and no one will be able to see Jesus because of the emotional wreckage in between Him and them—the wreckage called *us*. The dysfunctional processes that we cling to in order to keep an impression of success must be eradicated. And they must be eradicated quickly.

And this is where ditching the Christian*ish* only becomes reality if we are willing to make the toughest decision of all. We must truly deny ourselves. Truly die to our own reputations. We tend to think that taking up our crosses and following Jesus will give us superstar status, putting us on par with Christ and making us famous for our humility. The truth is that taking up our cross means taking on the ridicule the world heaps on Jesus. Taking on the unpopularity and the heap of misunderstandings and the blame and all of the damage and then heaping love back onto that abusing world.

It is the antithesis of what the world sees now (men and women discussing love while abusing one another): men and women pointing to Jesus while seizing the spotlight for themselves. The audiences of the world have already changed the channel off of the Jesus show because it does not ring true. In the process they have mistakenly believed that this is all there is to Jesus.

We have done this damage ourselves.

It is our Christian mission to set things right.

To get our own backstage in order so that we are loving one another and the world with the truth of Jesus Christ.

To tell the truth and the whole truth in love so that, even when unpopular, we will exemplify the reality of Christ to all who choose to listen.

To stop hogging the spotlight and the ovations and instead painfully stretch so that the world will finally be able to see Jesus and only Jesus ...

... because you and I will have finally stepped out of the way.

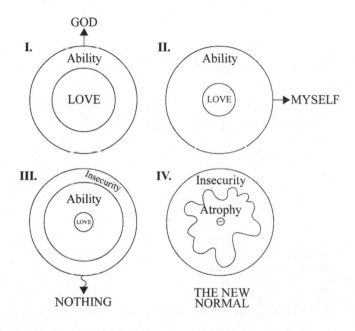

1. Why do we feel such a strong need to perform in order to "earn" our salvation? Is this a natural human urge, or is it cultural?

2. Have you ever been involved in a ministry project where, behind the scenes, there was strife and dissension? What was lost in the process?

3. What are some of the ways that a performance mentality robs our joy on the journey of ministry?

4. Pain is often required as a path to purpose. Why is this true? Have you experienced this truth?

5. Atrophied muscles require stretching. What muscles of your faith have atrophied? What sort of stretching will be required?

6. What happens when we take our God-given talents and abilities and serve ourselves instead of Him?

7. Performance mentality leads to lack of personal fulfillment, an absence of perspective, strife, personal chaos, and pain. Have you found this to be true?

8. Can you or your church relate to the thought "atrophy is the new normal"? Why?

9. Are you following Jesus or are you following applause? Can you think back on seasons of your life where each was accurate?

10. *"We only truly love the people in this world when we simultaneously risk unpopularity."* What do you think this means?

11. Have you ever done the correct *what* for the incorrect *why?*

in Jesus' name, amends 11

Michael was acrophobic.

This does not mean he was afraid of circus clowns. Rather, he was afraid of heights. Acrophobia is an irrational emotional condition characterized by an abnormal life-or-death fear of high places. It can be dangerous because when acrophobics experience heights, they often have panic attacks and are therefore incapable of climbing down to safety. This wouldn't have been such an extreme concern for me had Michael and I never met. But I didn't know he was an acrophobic. And it was my job to put him in the sky.

It was the spring of 1996 and Kaysie and I were leading summer mission teams through a ropes training course that was designed to help them build up teamwork skills while facing their individual fears head-on. It was the exact same training camp that I had attended myself five years earlier. Yeah, the one with the back pain and the stretching. The one with Andrea. Five years later she and I were working for the same company.

My wife and I were continually energized by bringing teams through the ropes challenge in the trees because we had been required to experience the same challenge ourselves at more fearful periods in our lives. That spring of 1991, a part of my student training had been to step into a harness, climb a telephone pole, and dive off the top of it in order to grab a trapeze. I had a minimal fear of heights myself, though I denied this. I felt it was ridiculous to be afraid of altitude. I was, however, terrified of hitting the ground after a lengthy fall. It wasn't the elevation that was frightening. It was the thudding afterward.

But I had been pushed to climb that telephone pole anyway—and twenty minutes later, when I was finally able to get my legs to stop shaking, I leapt off. This is what I considered a fear of heights.

Until I met Michael.

I was facilitating the team heading to England for the summer: a very astute, intellectual group—savvy with head knowledge and spiritual insight. Quiet, reserved. You can see why I was paired with them.

The schedule for the first day was simple enough. I was to lead the team through several ground elements. None were even slightly threatening. They were designed to test the group for rough spots in communication. Most of the day had passed and the team had fared well. So we began the late afternoon with the Trust Fall.

Simply stated, the Trust Fall is an exercise in which each team member takes turns falling backward into the arms of the remainder of the team. It is monitored and safe, and involves special stances and holds as well as verbal warnings and cues for the fall itself. When all is said and done, the faller falls delightfully into the arms of eight catchers.

I don't know exactly why it is called the Trust Fall because in this exercise, everyone falls, but very few trust. The few who do succeed in trusting are normally those who don't have much of an issue with touch or heights to begin with. For those, it is easy and therefore elicits growth only by forcing them to deal with others who have a more difficult time. Touch is the big issue here. If you have a body issue or an abuse issue, it is a great challenge to trust the arms of human beings. But if you have touch issues *and* height issues? Watch out. To this end, enter Michael.

Michael was thin and bookish—extremely quiet. Most on the team had taken him to be an extreme intellectual. Over the course of the day, I had witnessed a kindhearted and likeable individual who refrained from interacting much. When he submitted input, it was strong but rare. I was concerned for Michael on the Trust Fall because I knew that the team would only know when to catch Michael if he spoke up. And I had never heard Michael speak above a muted whisper.

As we worked our way through each member of the team, we faced the usual amount of trials and attitudes, and all the while Michael aided in catching each team member exactly as he had been instructed. And then it was his turn up on the platform.

The platform was only four feet off the ground. Not even the height of an average human being. It was not intended to be anxiety-high. It was only intended to be cold-sweat-high because the following two days would require these individuals to climb to greater and greater altitudes and we didn't want to scare anyone off the checkerboard on square one. I had seen a few people freeze up on this small wooden platform—I had seen more than a few brought to tears. But I had never experienced Michael.

I took Michael by the hand, helping him up to a platform the size of a cardboard box lid. He was all smiles, just as he had been all day long. He turned his back to face me, leaving his teammates and the ground out of his line of sight. His safety disappeared behind his back and along with it the Michael I had known. His eyes seemed to focus inward as his body shook. I knew instantly that something was gravely wrong. It is difficult to explain what happened to Michael's face at that moment, but it was as if he was suddenly aging backward. That fear in the eyes that you only see when a four-year-old first experiences a horrible car accident. The sudden disappearance of color that accompanies news of a loved one's death. The previous Michael evaporated, thrust into some other dimension. He reverted to the deepest fear I had ever seen manifest itself in someone's appearance. It was as if his body folded inward, becoming smaller.

As I repeated the words "Take the falling stance, Michael," it became evident that his mind was lost somewhere far away from the range of my voice. The sweat poured down his face and I was fairly certain that he was not completely aware of where he was or what was going on. I helped him get his bearings and made him look me straight in the eyes. This seemed to calm him enough to remind him of his instructions. His disciplined body kicked in and positioned itself as his team continued to encourage him. I saw a moment of determination in his eyes, and he thrust himself backward.

And then—right at the moment of the fall—that nanosecond where his body told him he should have been caught by now—Michael let out the loudest, most bloodcurdling scream I have ever heard in my life. He released a grieving expulsion of a moan so deeply startling that my soul hurt and for a moment I feared for his life.

But then he was caught.

The team stopped silent, surprised by his reaction. I stared at him from the ledge as he stared back, his wits coming back to him. His team set him down gently, standing him up and waiting on his silence. A few seconds went by—and then the emotion poured.

Michael wept. He wept as I had never seen a human weep. He wept as he himself had never wept—never grieved the deep-seated fear inside of him. At that moment, as unfamiliar emotions poured audibly out of Michael as he experienced them for the first time, he told us his story.

As a baby Michael had been set down in his crib for a nap while his mother worked out in the yard. Michael, however, had not fallen asleep. He wanted to be with his mother, so he attempted to climb out of the crib on his own. While climbing, his ankle caught in between the bars, and Michael hung, stuck upside-down, from the outside railing of the crib. He screamed and screamed until his lungs gave out, but no one was within earshot. When his family finally checked on him, he had been hanging upside down by his ankle for over two hours. He was silent and lethargic, having cried as long as his small body would allow. From that moment on Michael could not bear to exist in even the slightest of high places. In those moments he shut down completely, reverting to that moment in infancy. This is how Michael became an acrophobic.

Upon hearing his story, the tone of the team changed. This was the irony: Michael had never told anyone his weakness because it was exactly that. But when he finally spoke the words out loud, it not only began shattering the power his fear had over him—it also became a rallying point for Team England. Where the team had been rooted in misunderstanding one another and every member vying to be heard, it was suddenly about a common goal: Help Michael conquer his fear. And in revealing his shortcoming to his team, Michael received the thing he least expected: strength to change.

And the sun fell on the first day.

Michael was acrophobic—a fear of abnormal intensity. It could only be called ironic that Michael was the first to strap a harness around his waist on day two.

As day one had come to a close, Michael had asked us to talk him through the remaining two days of ropes courses. We described day two: the day spent in the trees. Each member on the team would be harnessed individually and would then maneuver his or her way solo through a forty-five-minute obstacle course two stories in the air. There would always be a counselor and an encourager close at hand to talk through the panic moments, but the safety of the individual would be in his own hands. Three times in the air he would be required to switch belays himself—a precarious position for someone prone to panic attacks. We suggested he remain on the ground. We considered day one's breakthrough quite enough.

But Michael would have nothing of it. Michael didn't want to just face his fear. He wanted to conquer it. To this end Michael asked Kaysie and me to encourage him from the ground. He also asked his team leader to follow the course in the trees behind him. He would be alone and he would feel alone—but he would be surrounded by support in the midst of it.

Kaysie and I had walked students through this course for years. We had seen people freak out before, though never half as intense. We had witnessed those who felt they were afraid of heights as they hugged trees, blaming whoever was in the way for their pain, and freezing to a standstill. We had seen whiners and complainers find all sorts of ways to blame nature and their team for their own unwillingness to change. But Michael was different. He was not a complainer. We all knew what was at stake. He needed to see this through—because seeing this through could change his entire life.

I strapped in Michael's buckles and double-checked them. I secured the harness and triple-checked it. I reassured Michael of all the safety elements he would have to remember. He asked a dozen questions, repeating most. He was hesitant. He was very afraid. Very, very afraid.

I told him it was time to climb. Michael looked upward, and it was clear that he was more afraid than I had ever seen anyone be afraid. Panic-stricken. The infant Michael resurfacing.

And then—Michael climbed anyway.

It took him twenty minutes to climb that first ladder. Those twelve steps to his personal hell—but he never stopped climbing. He simply moved one millimeter at a time. And as he reached the top of those trees, the most amazing thing happened. Michael was terrified. Michael struggled and cried out to God. He lost his balance and was filled with uncomfortable emotion. He didn't think he could succeed. But he never stopped.

Get this: Michael was literally suffering through his worst nightmare. Abject terror. And he never—I repeat—*never* froze. He moved methodically through every single step, accurately verbalizing all safety checks and balances while creeping through sheer fright. He never hugged a tree—never gave himself time to rationalize why he should give up. He embraced the pain. Every simmering, defeating nugget of pain. He sobbed. Literally yawped his way through inch upon inch. Tears streamed down his face (as well as ours) as he continually quoted Scripture to give his physical anguish some spiritual hope. He pushed on from element to element, taking three hours to complete the forty-five-minute course, physically alone all the while. He prayed. He focused. He wept. He was scared to death. But he never stopped.

My wife and I, as well as all who were watching, choked up as we witnessed a man looking solely to God to face the darkest challenge in his life—a deep, tainted side that I had not yet had to face myself. And where I had seen so many others with lesser challenges shrink back within themselves screaming, "I can't do this," here was a man who seemed weak but was so much stronger than any of us could have ever imagined.

Michael discovered his darkest place and faced it head-on. He refused to pause and remain on growth hiatus until his circumstances changed. He did not refuse to move until God made him braver. He stepped out when it could not have possibly been more difficult, becoming completely vulnerable to God to make good on His biblical promise that we can do all things through Him who gives us strength. He fell into the climb that he knew would heal him. And he never stopped. Not once did he cry, "I can't" or "I quit." He didn't second-guess God's conquering power. He simply submitted and responded accordingly and in the process turned his greatest tragedy into his greatest testimony.

In fact the true irony is that Michael became my hero that day. He became the hero for all of us—the last thing he would have ever expected to become. Not because he was flawless, but quite the contrary. Because he was willing to identify the flaw and relentlessly pursue healing through pain.

Michael finished the course in the trees and prepared to swing down. We all watched as this proclaimed acrophobic sat on a ledge forty feet above us, epitomizing a man of God. He knew this last push down off of the heights would be the most dramatic physical sensation of falling that he had experienced in the entire ordeal. The final pain would indeed be the most severe. But he also knew this first and worst trial would then be over.

He sat on the wood plank that held his harness in. His facilitator asked if he wanted to say anything. He wept as he looked to the skies, beyond the treeline—into the heavens—and whisper-screamed …

"for You."

The emotion welled in us all, and as he flung into the air to release his last bit of fear, the tears could no longer be contained in any of us.

As I unhooked Michael on the ground, there was a strength and a peace that I have rarely seen on a man's face. His pain was gone. Seriously. Gone. A lifetime of anxiety had been released through the sacrifice of a child of God. Michael's team rushed to his side, applauding and embracing. The remainder of spectators took their own whining into perspective and felt a lump in their throats. They rallied around him like a football hero, hailing his achievements after the championship game. He was the talk of the camp—except for Michael himself, of course. All evening, whenever I glanced his way, Michael was simply seated in silence—smiling.

And the sun fell on the second day.

Michael was acrophobic. But on the third day you would have never known it.

The team's final assignment was the aforementioned telephone pole and a thirty-foot rock-climbing wall. Michael completed them first, like a monkey born in the trees. All watched in stunned amazement at this changed man, a true testament to the delivering and healing power that God wields when one man radically submits that which he fears the most.

But that wasn't the most intriguing part of the change in Michael. On day three several other teams joined together. And many of those teams had not seen the same triumph in themselves that Team England had experienced so dramatically. In fact many of those teams were in such a struggling state that certain members of the team did not consider themselves courageous enough to even attempt the pole. When those people faltered due to fear, who did they request as their encourager?

Michael.

All day long Michael helped individuals work past their weaknesses and push far—farther than they considered possible. They trusted him—not because they observed Michael's perfection or because he had the correct self-help catchphrase. They trusted Michael because they had observed his flaw, and what he had chosen to do with it. They witnessed a man who had not waited on change in himself in order to act. He had not waited for his knees to stop shaking. Instead, he expected Christ to remain solid as a rock.

Michael spent that entire summer in England, spreading the gospel of Jesus Christ, but he had already been a missionary to many. Michael had an entire summer to find brand-new adjectives to describe himself and replace the one he had worn for twenty-four years.

Michael used to be an acrophobic.

But Michael abandoned that word in the trees.

Now Michael is an overcomer.

THE PERSON IS SCARY

The modern church loves Michael's story—because Michael is a mover. Michael pushed progress forward, continually advancing. This is exactly what the modern church would prefer to look like, and to us on the inside, we do. We gaze at all the programs and the outreaches and the ministry opportunities that our hard work—our perpetual inching forward—has wrought. To this end, all of us on the inside of the American church would characterize ourselves as Michaels: as those who forge on against the odds with no fear, running the race to win the prize.

Unfortunately, to those outside the church, we just look like a bunch of tree huggers. Frozen in our tracks, incapable of advancing. Allowing the deepest fears and the core issues to go untreated while we grow so catatonic that we can barely move. From the world's perspective the American church has been unwieldy, slow to push forward. But from our own perspective we are accomplishing more than ever. Why is there this disconnect?

It does not merely come down to what we have done. It comes down to the world's perception of why. To us, larger buildings are a means to better serve a community. Events and rallies, programs and outreaches—all of these efforts are to make ministry tangible to the senses: an attempt to bring Jesus to those who would not set foot inside a church. Christian television, Christian film, Christian books (and on and on and on) are means by which we throw the Word out there expecting it to not return void. For the most part we're a rather well-intentioned lot.

But as our reach has grown, our brand has smacked more and more sour. To an unchurched world, they will never see the good intentions behind such efforts. They accept instead what their senses tell them to accept. They see more bombast and they assume artificial. They observe the message being thinned out to reach the largest demographic and they assume shallow profiteering. They see the Christian brand growing larger, and they assume what is unfortunately true: that we are mastering mass communication, but we are scared to death of the intimately personal. It appears to those on the outside that we cater to the masses by remaining on the surface rather than investing in the individual by digging deep.

Christian teaching has exploded in the last twenty years—but in many ways, not for the better. It has been watered down to daily, simple, self-improvement blurbs. Desk-calendar Christianity. Sound-bite sermonizing. It sells a lot of books. It makes a great tagline for a film that will prove churchgoers attend movies. It will even bring in record-breaking donations if enough elderly call the number on the television screen. But it does not work its way into the painful places of the heart. It doesn't work for the people who have questions and are already of the belief that we do not have any answers handy. Through both the vastness of our methods and the reduced nature of our message, we have communicated (whether wittingly or unwittingly) that we are anxious to have a large audience, but not necessarily complete converts. We are prepared to be successful, but not very anxious to get intimate.

It is this mass-message approach that is completely redefining Jesus in the eyes of our nation and the world. We have gravitated more toward finding those who already think the way we do and ushering them into our church *(ideology-hugging)* instead of finding those who vehemently disagree with us and clarifying the truth of Christ *(ideology-transforming)*. Let's face it: *Ideology-hugging* is easier. It requires fewer financial resources and it has a much higher success rate. It makes for a church filled with excited people who all rally around the same philosophical bent. It feels good, and you don't have to get all that deep because the reason those people are at church in the first place is to have a group with which to agree. It's not preaching to the choir. It's building a church that consists only of the choir.

Ideology-transforming is far more challenging. It is never successful quickly. It requires tenaciousness, depth of understanding, intense vulnerability, empathy for those who disagree, and a willingness to be humbled. Not exactly the reason a people-pleaser gets into ministry to begin with. The type of person who requires *ideology-transforming* seems like too much work. He or she is the disillusioned American who despises or resents the church because of his or her misunderstanding of what the church is supposed to be. His or her theology, politics, societal thinking—all of it ruffles the feathers of the average churchgoer. To truly introduce this individual to Jesus, it would require a great amount of relational investment, a confident grasp of Scripture, and an affection for the child of God that he or she is (even if he or she refuses to acknowledge that fact). The process is painful. The process is untested. And to the church that person is scary.

So instead we only fulfill portions of the Great Commission by sending teams overseas or into the inner city. But as far as entering a relationship and a conversation with someone who needs and deserves *ideology-transformation*? Well—we hug the tree.

We may not have a phobia about heights, but we certainly have one about depth.

We hesitate to engage with an antagonistic culture because we perceive it as the problem. We believe, *If the rest of America would just get their act together, we wouldn't be this cesspool of immorality.* But the adverse is more accurate: *If the church would get its act together in regard to how we communicate Jesus to the rest of America, the spiral would stop edging downward.* We aren't strategically considering how the unchurched feel, what the unchurched think. We certainly aren't reasoning through the Christian*ish* things we have done and said that have steered them the wrong way.

We don't relate truth. We react to untruth. We don't like that they don't like us, so we unintentionally devalue their hurts and needs. We stop seeing them as reachable. And when we stop seeing someone as reachable, we stop seeing him or her as human. Suddenly our statements become about proving ourselves accurate—a counterattack to amorality and immorality instead of a loving courtship wooing someone away from sin.

The truth is far more complex, and will require much more out of us if we want to be truly Christian. If we want to be Christian*ish*, then it is enough to pick sides, alienating those who disagree with us even more by devaluing what they have to say on a daily basis. But if we want to be like Jesus, we have to be more tactical in the way we chip through the misconceptions (both theirs and our own) in order to truly make disciples of all men.

All men.

That is what Jesus said when He left this planet. At the very end of His life of ministry, He stood before all those who believed Him enough to follow Him to His exiting place. He gave them a few last words:

> *Then the eleven disciples went to Galilee, to the mountain where Jesus had told them to go. When they saw him, they worshiped him; but some doubted. Then Jesus came to them and said, "All authority in heaven and on earth has been given to me. Therefore go and make disciples of all nations, baptizing them in the name of the Father and of the Son and of the Holy Spirit, and teaching them to obey everything I have commanded you. And surely I am with you always, to the very end of the age."*
>
> Matthew 28:16–20

All nations. All men. All women. Everyone. Not just the nations that you do not call home. Not only the people that you will never see again. Jesus called us to reach them all—and not only *"reach,"* but *"make disciples."* It is our mandate as true Christians to help all men and women discover the deep reality of who Jesus is. Absorb this. It is not only our responsibility to pass on facts. It is our responsibility to help those facts become immersed into lifestyle. Nowhere is this more challenging than in the lives of those whom Christianity has turned off by our bad fact-stating habits. Truth will never be perceived as truth if it is not first drowned in love. Without love, truth appears as merely dogma. And in modern culture everyone is quick to kick the dogma.

It is this "disciple-making" that freezes us up—keeps us hugging the tree. We make great strides in reaching those who are pretty much already willing to make a decision for Christ, but we shy away from those who knock us: the news media, the political left, the entertainment industry, the homosexual community, the postmodern generation. We interface with them only in ugly debate. We lead the conversation with the differences in our thinking instead of with the similarities of our spiritual needs. In this approach we make the morality of Christ crystal clear, but we sift all of the love out of that morality. We stand on our arguments to gain a few inches of superiority instead of humbling ourselves to wash a sinner's feet. Isn't that what Christ did? Serve even those who did not yet understand? Isn't that what He commanded us to do? Love our enemies. Pray for those who persecute us. Not only for what it does to us— but for what it does to them.

It is no wonder that right before Jesus gave this Great Commission, the disciples are described as such: *"They worshiped him; but some doubted."* Wow. Even the eleven that stuck through Jesus' entire earthly ministry—after all was said and done and the resurrection proven true—even then some of them kept hugging that tree.

I suppose this "making disciples of all nations" idea isn't supposed to be easy.

We gaze at the world around us, and we are quick to complain that it is headed in the wrong direction. We observe the people of this nation who are our polar opposites, and instead of embracing them, we shun them as antagonists—as obstacles in the way of the gospel. We excuse that we feel this way because we believe they first shunned us.

But they weren't given the Great Commission. We were.

We can complain all we want about the liberalization of America. But we did it. We did it because we thought all our ideas were the truth and therefore we would win. To this end we didn't embrace. We spat. We didn't love. We soapboxed. We didn't attempt to understand them. We were just deeply offended when they didn't understand us.

It's time to let go of that tree.

And though at times it may feel like we are kicking and screaming to make mere inches of progress, we must forge through the brush and the chaos that we have helped create. We cannot give up on those who currently oppose Jesus. Because Jesus has not given up on them—and we are the only bridge through which they might first discover His love.

We must humble ourselves before Christ and ask Him to soften our hearts toward those in this world who have offended us. We must surrender to Jesus' love for *them*. We must swallow our pride and keep pushing through the obstacle course until freedom bursts forth at the end of the line. In that moment, in our humility and honesty, it will not only be our tears that have changed us.

Those watching will be changed as well.

This world, this nation, this culture—they will only be transformed for Jesus if we make the first move. We must answer the

Great Commission in its entirety. We must step down off of our soapboxes and love those whom we have deemed so unlovable. It will change them—and, oh yes, it will change us.

In Jesus' name—it is time to make amends.

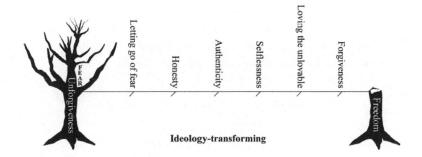

1.   Michael had never told anyone about his acrophobia, but when he finally spoke the words out loud, it not only began shattering the power his fear had over him—it also became a rallying point for the team. Have you ever seen fear broken by being honest about weakness?

2.   In revealing his shortcoming to his team, Michael received the thing he least expected: strength to change. Do you believe this is true? Does making weakness known bring strength? How?

3.   Why do we keep our weaknesses secret?

4.   Michael refused to pause and remain on growth hiatus until his circumstances changed. He stepped out when it could not have possibly been more difficult. Why do we resist moving forward in these same moments?

5.   Michael was a hero because he was willing to identify his flaw and relentlessly pursue healing through pain. Discuss why this ministers to others so deeply.

6.   In three days' time, Michael went from fear ruling his life to facing his fear head-on to helping others face their own fears. Three days, after a lifetime of pain. Why do we cling to fear and pain when facing it could lead to such healing?

7.   What does it look like to radically submit what you fear the most?

8. Why does the world's perception of "why the church does what it does" matter?

9. *"The modern church is mastering mass communication, but is scared to death of the intimately personal. It appears to those on the outside that we cater to the masses by remaining on the surface rather than investing in the individual by digging deep."* In what ways have you found this to be true? In what ways has your local church body done a good job at getting intimately personal?

10. Is your personal faith walk characterized more by *ideology-hugging* or *ideology-transforming?*

11. *Ideology-transforming* requires tenaciousness, depth of understanding, intense vulnerability, empathy for those who disagree, and a willingness to be humbled. Are we ready to take this approach to ministry? Why or why not?

12. *"Truth will never be perceived as truth if it is not first drowned in love. Without love, truth appears as merely dogma."* Agree or disagree?

i am Christian

So our lives indeed have sharp edges.

They hold the ability to perform life-altering surgery while retaining the risk of inflicting massive wounds. It all comes down to how we choose to wield the blades. This intentional act is a massive responsibility. It is a challenging manner in which to live—but it is the only path that leads to healing—for others as well as ourselves.

The only alternative is a life of fast food.

For something as simple as fast food, the burger chains certainly do get it wrong a lot. It would seem that the ordering of three specific items would not be enough to max out even the tiniest of tweener brains. This is why, when you order a number three burger, gargantua-sized with a diet soda, you feel it is safe to trust the eleven-year-old at the window enough that you don't unfold the crease at the top of the sack until you are back on the road. That is precisely the moment when you discover the fish sandwich in the place of your number three burger. And it isn't even gargantua.

And yet I continue to frequent the drive-through window for the sake of speed and convenience. Though it is rarely accurate, barely tasty, and never healthy, I somehow continue to give in to the urge that hasty and filling garbage is better than having to wait for slow-cooked nourishment.

It must be this precise line of reasoning that prompted me to consider purchasing a bottle of water from my hotel room's cash bar.

Before you comment, I do completely understand that there were bottles of water in the vending machine just outside in the hallway, or perhaps one or two floors down. I understand that the bottle of water in the microfridge under the table next to my bed was at least three times the vending machine bottle's price. You've got to be staring at a fairly hefty price tag if you consider the one-dollar bottle of water a comparative bargain. But gosh darn if my little personal fridge wasn't a heck of a lot more convenient. And there were candy bars and almonds and little bags of pumpkin seeds so overpriced that they just had to be autographed by Stephen Baldwin.

The cash bar required a key. A key that I had been given at check-in. This insinuated that I was elite—chosen specifically to be trusted with a purchase from the minikitchen tucked 'neath my nightstand. I was not merely purchasing refreshment—I was confirming the status that I alone was trustworthy enough to receive the hotel snack key.

I reasoned carefully through my options. I needed water and I refused to drink from the tap, having acquired a parasite years prior by doing that very thing. My choices were clear: three dollars for a bottle of water in the locked fridge nine inches from my hand—or one dollar for the bottle of water a hundred feet away that I would have to put on my shoes to retrieve down the long, dark hallway.

Gourmet water wins!

I savored the bottle, convincing myself it had a subtle spearmint taste that merited the 200 percent tip. However, about two-thirds of the way through, the haunting began.

Buyer's remorse.

I was clearly insane. Had I merely rounded the corner, I would have discovered three bottles of the same water for the price of the one purchased. So why did I do it? To live vicariously wealthy? To feel the thrill of the elite purchase? Or was I simply too lazy to care?

The truth is, I am often faced with two roads: the difficult path—and the costly, easy path. The surgery—or the damage. The Christian path—or the Christian*ish*.

I resist the hard path knowing full and well by experience that it is the hard path that has always changed me (and others) for the better. It is the walk down the long, dark hallway that has often created an unexpected side trip to the answer I had been searching for elsewhere. In a world that craves instant answers, it is through sweat, tears, and patience that we become the type of people who actually recognize the answers when we see them.

And yet for most of my life, I persisted on the Christian*ish* path.

I am finally starting to have some serious buyer's remorse.

I am realizing that the patient, healthy approach is the only option worthwhile.

HE DID MORE

A few years ago my wife, Kaysie, began to have some severe pain in her abdomen, so she went to the doctor to be examined. Aware of all the bizarre maladies that have occurred in our family, we broached the checkup with hesitation. Our mouths were saying *it's nothing* while that acidic portion of the stomach that tends to do somersaults was saying something else entirely.

Our hearts sank as the doctor told Kaysie that he had discovered a mass.

Anyone who has gone through this process understands the concern and frustration. No single practitioner seems to be able to identify the nature of the mass on his or her own. They keep passing the information buck. Hence, Kaysie had to go back and forth between too many doctors for all sorts of examinations to determine the root. Until someone came up with a solution, we would have no idea whether or not the mass was large or small, dangerous or innocuous. And the delayed scheduling (and delayed answers) meant our anxiety was given great breathing room to grow.

We prayed fervently—*Father, please take this thing away.* But every time Kaysie visited a doctor, they each saw the same mass. Though none of them were able to give us an answer in regard to its intention. This caused the invader in Kaysie's body to seem foreign and scary, in the shadows. What exactly was sneaking up inside of her?

It was finally determined that Kaysie would need surgery to remove the mass, regardless of what it was, because it appeared to be growing.

Growing? This was disturbing, to say the least.

We realized we only had two options remaining: to fear or to pray.

We prayed more earnestly. And then, as we discussed the next steps, Kaysie said the most powerful thing: She said that she suddenly had peace.

The reason this is so extraordinary is because Kaysie and I both have a repressed doomsday nature, where we continually have to work to have faith to stave off concerns of the imagined worst. We also have a desperate need for answers, and this scenario would require a radical decision without any. The battle of the mind is our most challenging and most crucial battle in the area of faith. It was an area that Kaysie and I had been striving to change. To realize that peace could reign even in the moment of utmost uncertainty, that God was worthy of our trust—even in the center of the crisis—represented enormous growth.

Growth that could not have happened had the mass disappeared at the beginning of the process.

We determined that we would trust God for a clean procedure where all of the mass would be removed and for rapid healing post-surgery.

The possibility never even crossed our minds that when Kaysie went in for her final checkup before the procedure, the doctor would find absolutely nothing.

But that's exactly what he found.

As if there had never even been a mass there to begin with.

Not a trace.

It was gone.

Kaysie broke the news to me—and our jaws just dropped.

Not because we didn't believe God could do this, but because we had not thought to ask Him to. We had asked Him to give us wisdom on how to proceed, or to make the mass safe. Instead He did more.

God had done more—actually *more* than we had asked or imagined—just like His Word says He will do. But He did it in His own timing instead of ours. He gave us answers *after* a hard, painful path. He did not solve our dilemma before it tested our faith and stretched us to better, stronger places. He allowed us to learn to be patient—to strengthen our trust.

After the climb in the frightening heights of the trees.

After the long, dark hallway walk to the water.

After the mass had started to grow.

He could have brought the trees lower to the ground. He could have given us the water the moment we asked for it, just a few inches from our hands. He could have eradicated the mass before we even found it. But that experience would have been fast food. It could not have changed us at all.

And we now live on the other side of that healing as stronger people with a faith proven true.

THE NEW NORMAL

The truth is, our Christian*ish* path will only give way to following Christ when we determine that we are each willing to take the slower, more painful, more developmental approach to our daily life. It comes when we are willing to go through the rough stuff for the purpose of being transformed. When we not only do the right thing, but do it in the way that observes, includes, and heals the hurting who stand alongside us. For too long modern Christianity has looked like fast food: the quickest, Bible-based shortcut to solutions and success—but in the process we are missing the parts of the journey that make us people of depth. We are dodging the lengthier routes that welcome others into our healing. But that route should become our new path.

It should become our new normal.

> *Are we beginning to commend ourselves again? Or do we need, like some people, letters of recommendation to you or from you? You yourselves are our letter, written on our hearts, known and read by everybody. You show that you are a letter from Christ, the result of our ministry, written not with ink but with the Spirit of the living God, not on tablets of stone but on tablets of human hearts.*
>
> 2 Corinthians 3:1–3

Like it or not, you and I are a letter of recommendation from Jesus. To this end the outcome of our lives is not the only thing that matters. Our salvation is not merely about our moment of surrender and our date of expiration. It is in fact all the words and deeds and actions and love and observable moments in between. All the tangible expressions of gratitude for God's grace. Our lives are ministry. Every moment is ministry. And ministry is surgery.

It's time to remove the cancer.

To eradicate selfishness and allow our painful transitions from Christian*ish* to godliness to be seen. To share the rough stuff. To watch our words and to develop patience. To stop performing and to refuse to waste grace.

And most of all to continually love.

I am no theologian. The only credential I have for writing a book like this is that I have made every mistake inside of it. I have not fully lived out any of the discoveries between these pages—but Jesus is speaking and I am listening.

Listening past the persuasion of culture.

Listening past the habits of the church.

Listening past my own preferences and emotions.

Whenever confusion erupts in my daily Christian walk—I go back to Jesus.

And that is the key of which I am certain. When I am *uncertain*, I go back to Jesus. I go to His words, His sentiments, His actions.

Not my own emotions.

Not my own reasoning.

Not public opinion.

Not the Sunday sermon.

Not the words in this book.

I go back to Jesus.

For forty years I leaned on my own understanding. That only led to chaos and confusion. I now determine to stop picking and choosing the aspects of my belief system that feed my obesity best.

Instead I will take my time and absorb the words and deeds of my Savior.

I will search desperately for His footsteps.

Because He is the one I will forever follow …

… as I finally leave that which is Christian*ish* behind.